LLEWELLYN'S 2026

Sabbats
ALMANAC

Samhain 2025
to
Mabon 2026

Llewellyn's 2026 Sabbats Almanac
Samhain 2025 to Mabon 2026

Cover art © Carolyn Vibbert
Editing by Hanna Grimson
Interior Art © Carolyn Vibbert, except on pages 13, 40, 79, 81, 114, 116, 154, 191, 201, 227, 261, 298, which are by the Llewellyn Art Department

You can order annuals and books from *New Worlds*, Llewellyn's catalog. To request a free copy, call 1-877-NEW WRLD toll-free or order online by visiting our website at http://subscriptions.llewellyn.com.

ISBN: 978-0-7387-7526-5

The publisher and the author assume no liability for any injuries caused to the reader that may result from the reader's use of content contained in this publication and recommend common sense when contemplating the practices described in the work.

Published by Llewellyn Worldwide Ltd.
2143 Wooddale Drive
Woodbury, MN 55125-2989
www.llewellyn.com

Printed in China

2025

JANUARY
S	M	T	W	T	F	S
			1	2	3	4
5	6	7	8	9	10	11
12	13	14	15	16	17	18
19	20	21	22	23	24	25
26	27	28	29	30	31	

FEBRUARY
S	M	T	W	T	F	S
						1
2	3	4	5	6	7	8
9	10	11	12	13	14	15
16	17	18	19	20	21	22
23	24	25	26	27	28	

MARCH
S	M	T	W	T	F	S
						1
2	3	4	5	6	7	8
9	10	11	12	13	14	15
16	17	18	19	20	21	22
23	24	25	26	27	28	29
30	31					

APRIL
S	M	T	W	T	F	S
		1	2	3	4	5
6	7	8	9	10	11	12
13	14	15	16	17	18	19
20	21	22	23	24	25	26
27	28	29	30			

MAY
S	M	T	W	T	F	S
				1	2	3
4	5	6	7	8	9	10
11	12	13	14	15	16	17
18	19	20	21	22	23	24
25	26	27	28	29	30	31

JUNE
S	M	T	W	T	F	S
1	2	3	4	5	6	7
8	9	10	11	12	13	14
15	16	17	18	19	20	21
22	23	24	25	26	27	28
29	30					

JULY
S	M	T	W	T	F	S
		1	2	3	4	5
6	7	8	9	10	11	12
13	14	15	16	17	18	19
20	21	22	23	24	25	26
27	28	29	30	31		

AUGUST
S	M	T	W	T	F	S
					1	2
3	4	5	6	7	8	9
10	11	12	13	14	15	16
17	18	19	20	21	22	23
24	25	26	27	28	29	30
31						

SEPTEMBER
S	M	T	W	T	F	S
	1	2	3	4	5	6
7	8	9	10	11	12	13
14	15	16	17	18	19	20
21	22	23	24	25	26	27
28	29	30				

OCTOBER
S	M	T	W	T	F	S
			1	2	3	4
5	6	7	8	9	10	11
12	13	14	15	16	17	18
19	20	21	22	23	24	25
26	27	28	29	30	31	

NOVEMBER
S	M	T	W	T	F	S
						1
2	3	4	5	6	7	8
9	10	11	12	13	14	15
16	17	18	19	20	21	22
23	24	25	26	27	28	29
30						

DECEMBER
S	M	T	W	T	F	S
	1	2	3	4	5	6
7	8	9	10	11	12	13
14	15	16	17	18	19	20
21	22	23	24	25	26	27
28	29	30	31			

2026

JANUARY
S	M	T	W	T	F	S
				1	2	3
4	5	6	7	8	9	10
11	12	13	14	15	16	17
18	19	20	21	22	23	24
25	26	27	28	29	30	31

FEBRUARY
S	M	T	W	T	F	S
1	2	3	4	5	6	7
8	9	10	11	12	13	14
15	16	17	18	19	20	21
22	23	24	25	26	27	28

MARCH
S	M	T	W	T	F	S
1	2	3	4	5	6	7
8	9	10	11	12	13	14
15	16	17	18	19	20	21
22	23	24	25	26	27	28
29	30	31				

APRIL
S	M	T	W	T	F	S
			1	2	3	4
5	6	7	8	9	10	11
12	13	14	15	16	17	18
19	20	21	22	23	24	25
26	27	28	29	30		

MAY
S	M	T	W	T	F	S
					1	2
3	4	5	6	7	8	9
10	11	12	13	14	15	16
17	18	19	20	21	22	23
24	25	26	27	28	29	30
31						

JUNE
S	M	T	W	T	F	S
	1	2	3	4	5	6
7	8	9	10	11	12	13
14	15	16	17	18	19	20
21	22	23	24	25	26	27
28	29	30				

JULY
S	M	T	W	T	F	S
			1	2	3	4
5	6	7	8	9	10	11
12	13	14	15	16	17	18
19	20	21	22	23	24	25
26	27	28	29	30	31	

AUGUST
S	M	T	W	T	F	S
						1
2	3	4	5	6	7	8
9	10	11	12	13	14	15
16	17	18	19	20	21	22
23	24	25	26	27	28	29
30	31					

SEPTEMBER
S	M	T	W	T	F	S
		1	2	3	4	5
6	7	8	9	10	11	12
13	14	15	16	17	18	19
20	21	22	23	24	25	26
27	28	29	30			

OCTOBER
S	M	T	W	T	F	S
				1	2	3
4	5	6	7	8	9	10
11	12	13	14	15	16	17
18	19	20	21	22	23	24
25	26	27	28	29	30	31

NOVEMBER
S	M	T	W	T	F	S
1	2	3	4	5	6	7
8	9	10	11	12	13	14
15	16	17	18	19	20	21
22	23	24	25	26	27	28
29	30					

DECEMBER
S	M	T	W	T	F	S
		1	2	3	4	5
6	7	8	9	10	11	12
13	14	15	16	17	18	19
20	21	22	23	24	25	26
27	28	29	30	31		

Contents

Ostara

Beltane

Litha

Lammas

Mabon

Introduction

NEARLY EVERYONE HAS A favorite sabbat. There are numerous ways to observe any tradition. The 2025 edition of the *Sabbats Almanac* provides a wealth of lore, celebrations, creative projects, and recipes to enhance your holiday.

For this edition, a mix of writers—Emma Kathryn, Dodie Graham McKay, Irene Glasse, Nathan M. Hall, Ben Stimpson, and more—share their ideas and wisdom. These include a variety of paths as well as the authors' personal approaches to each sabbat. Each chapter closes with an extended ritual, which may be adapted for both solitary practitioners and covens.

In addition to these insights and rituals, specialists in astrology, cooking, crafts, and more impart their expertise throughout.

Michael Herkes gives an overview of planetary influences most relevant for each sabbat season and provides details about the New and Full Moons, retrograde motion, planetary positions, and more. (Times and dates follow Eastern Standard Time and Eastern Daylight Time.)

Tomás Prower explores stories and myths from around the world and how they connect to each sabbat.

Nathan M. Hall conjures up a feast for each festival that features seasonal appetizers, entrées, beverages, and desserts.

Raechel Henderson offers instructions on DIY crafts that will help you tap into each sabbat's energy and fill your home with magic and fun.

Elizabeth Barrette provides meditations to utilize the unique forces in each season.

About the Authors

Elizabeth Barrette has been involved with the Pagan community for more than thirty-five years. She served as managing editor of *PanGaia* for eight years and dean of studies at the Grey School of Wizardry for four years. She has written columns on beginning and intermediate Pagan practice, Pagan culture, and Pagan leadership. Her book *Composing Magic: How to Create Magical Spells, Rituals, Blessings, Chants, and Prayers* explains how to combine writing and spirituality. She lives in central Illinois, where she has done much networking with Pagans in her area, such as coffeehouse meetings and open sabbats. Her other public activities feature Pagan picnics and science fiction conventions. She enjoys magical crafts, historic religions, and gardening for wildlife. Her other writing fields include speculative fiction, gender studies, and social and environmental issues. Visit her blog, *The Wordsmith's Forge* (https://ysabetwordsmith .dreamwidth.org/), or website PenUltimate Productions (http:// penultimateproductions.weebly.com). Her coven site with extensive Pagan materials is Greenhaven Tradition (http://greenhaventradition .weebly.com/).

Jenny C. Bell (she/her) is a spiritual witch who has walked this path for over thirty years. Jenny loves the reclaiming of the word *witch* and believes anyone and everyone could be a witch. She is a spiritual Jill of all trades with a background in yoga, meditation, tarot, crystal healing, Reiki, channeling, and herbal remedies. Jenny is the founder of Our Coven, an inclusive international online community of witches and spiritual folks. She lives in the PNW with her family and pets where she practices as a stay-at-home fortune teller, creator, and writer. You can find out more about Jenny at jennycbell .com.

Irene Glasse is a Heathen witch based in Western Maryland. She is a longtime teacher of witchcraft, meditation, and magic in the mid-Atlantic. She is the coauthor of *Blackfeather Mystery School: The Magpie Training* (Dragon Alchemy, 2022), a contributing writer for *Gemini Witch: Unlock the Magic of Your Sun Sign* and *Llewellyn's 2024 and 2025 Sabbats Almanac* (Llewellyn, 2023 and 2024), and a blogger and columnist. Irene has performed, taught workshops, and led rituals at many festivals and conferences over the years. She is the main organizer of the Frederick Covenant of Unitarian Universalist Pagans (Frederick CUUPS), offering events, rituals, classes, and workshops to a large, vibrant community.

Nathan M. Hall is an animist and witch who lives in South Florida. His book, *Path of the Moonlit Hedge*, is available wherever books are sold. Find him online at moonlithedge.com.

Raechel Henderson is a dual class seamstress/shieldmaiden. She is the author of *Sew Witchy: Tools, Techniques & Projects for Sewing Magick* as well as *The Scent of Lemon & Rosemary: Working Domestic Magick with Hestia*, both from Llewellyn Worldwide. You can find her on Instagram, Facebook, or at her blog (idiorhythmic.com) where she writes about magick, creativity, living by one's own life patterns, her family, and books.

Michael Herkes (aka The Glam Witch) makes magic across the windy city of Chicago as a genderqueer author, astrologer, intuitive stylist, tarot reader, and glamour witch. After practicing privately for two decades, Michael stepped out of the broom closet and into the role of teacher—dedicating their energy to uplifting and mentoring others on using witchcraft for self-empowerment. Since then, they have authored numerous books, written a variety of digital content, and presented workshops across the United States as a speaker on modern witchcraft. Focusing primarily on glamour magic, Michael's practice centers on magical aesthetics and adornment, using fashion and makeup to cultivate inner and outer makeovers—inspiring others to tap into their personal power and creativity to manifest positive change in their lives and the world around them. For more information visit www.theglamwitch.com.

Emma Kathryn (Nottinghamshire, UK) is a staff writer at *Witch Way Magazine*, *The House of Twigs* blog, *Stone, Root, and Bone* blog, the *Spiral Nature* blog, and *Gods & Radicals*. She hosts *Wild Witch Podcast* and has spoken at several UK Pagan events, including Magickal Women Conference in London. Visit her online at www.EmmaKathrynWildWitchcraft.com.

Lupa is a naturalist Pagan author and artist in the Pacific Northwest. She is the author of several books on nature-based Paganism and is the creator of the Tarot of Bones. Her work may be found at http://www.thegreenwolf.com.

Dodie Graham McKay is a writer, Green Witch, Gardnerian priestess, and filmmaker. She is inspired to document and share stories that capture the beauty of nature and the visible and invisible realms of magic and witchcraft. She is the author of the books *Earth Magic: Elements of Witchcraft* (Llewellyn, 2021), *A Witch's Ally: Building a Magical Relationship with Animal Familiars & Companions* (Llewellyn, 2024), and her documentary films include *The WinniPagans* and *Starry Nights* (featuring Kerr Cuhulain), and the four-part series *Exploring the Sacred*. Dodie spends her spare time walking her dogs and facilitating a busy coven. She lives in Treaty One Territory, Homeland of the Red River Métis Nation, Winnipeg, Manitoba, Canada. Visit her at www.dodiegrahammckay.com.

Sara Mellas is a writer, musician, and psychic astrologer living in Nashville, Tennessee. She's authored four books and has written about music, astrology, metaphysics, and kitchen arts for several publications. In addition to writing, she offers private psychic and astrological readings and works as a commercial food stylist. She spends her free time as the primary songwriter and lead singer for the rock band Miele and can usually be found with a canine friend by her side. Her website is www.saramellas.com; to book a reading, visit www.calendly.com/sara-saramellas.

Tomás Prower is the award-winning Latinx author of books on multicultural magic and mysticism, including *Queer Magic* and *Morbid Magic*. Fluent in English, French, and Spanish, he previously served as the cultural liaison between France, the United States, and various nations of South America, which allowed him to live and work all over the Western Hemisphere, including Buenos Aires, Santiago de Chile, Tijuana, Reno, Las Vegas, and the Amazon jungle. Tomás is also a licensed mortuary professional and former External Relations Director of the American Red Cross. Visit him at TomasPrower.com.

Ben Stimpson is an award-winning author, therapist, spiritual practitioner, educator, and folklorist located in the United Kingdom. He holds a bachelors of liberal studies from the University of Waterloo (Waterloo, Ontario), where he minored in classical, medieval, and religious studies. He is the author of *Ancestral Whispers: A Guide to Building Ancestral Veneration Practices* (Llewellyn, 2023) a COVR gold award-winning title, and *Wise Ones: Legends of Witches, Magicians and Cunning Folk of England and Wales* (Crossed Crow Books, 2025). Coming from a diverse spiritual background, Ben has had previous experiences with Hinduism, Lukumi, espiritismo, Druidry, and British folk tradition. When not writing, Ben hosts the semi-regular podcast *Essence*, where he interviews fellow authors in the occult, metaphysical, and Neopagan niche. To find out more about Ben, please visit www.benstimpson.com.

Charlie Rainbow Wolf is an old hippie who's been studying the weird ways of the world for over fifty years. She's happiest when she's got her hands in mud, either making pottery in the "artbox" or tending to things in the yarden (yard + garden = yarden). Astrology, tarot, and herbs are her greatest interests, but she's dabbled in most metaphysical topics in the last five decades because life always has something new to offer. She enjoys cooking WFPB recipes and knitting traditional cables and patterns, and she makes a wicked batch of fudge. Charlie lives in central Illinois with her very patient husband and her beloved Great Danes.

Samhain

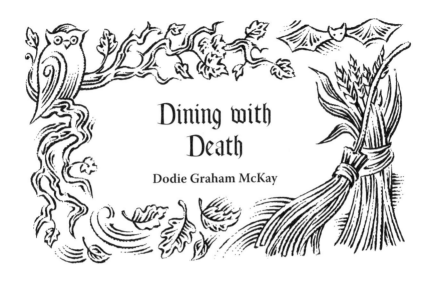

Dining with Death

Dodie Graham McKay

THE DAYS ARE BECOMING shorter, the nights are getting cooler, the shadows are growing darker—this can only mear that Samhain is drawing near. This is the season that comes at the end of the growth and abundance of the harvest, when the life cycle of the crops comes to an end and we see the imminence of death reflected in the decay of the plant life around us. We sense our own mortality and our impending connection to the mystery of what is beyond our own life.

The sabbat of Samhain is often celebrated on October 31 (or April 30/May 1 in the Southern Hemisphere), right alongside secular Halloween celebrations. Many witch and Pagan folk like to spread out the tide of the season and hold sabbat celebrations on the closest weekend to the end of October (or April in the Southern Hemisphere). Samhain marks the midway point between the Autumn Equinox and Winter Solstice and is sometimes referred to as a *cross-quarter day*.

My own coven started celebrating Samhain on the actual cross-quarter day, which usually falls five to seven days into November (or May in the Southern Hemisphere), as we like to separate the fun of Halloween and the spiritual nature of Samhain. Dividing up the celebrations this way also accommodated the parents in the group, who were able to take their kids out trick-or-treating and then attend our Samhain sabbat celebrations and enjoy both things fully. The actual date you choose is up to you; the important thing is to *do* something that is meaningful to you and the people you choose to celebrate with.

A Time for Death

Death is a theme that is intimately linked with this time of year. Many believe that Samhain is a liminal time, when the veil between our world and the world of spirits is at its thinnest, allowing for connection and communication to flow more easily between us and our beloved and mighty dead. The *beloved dead* were the people in our lives—family, friends, acquaintances—who we actually knew who have died. The *mighty dead* refers to people we admired from afar and may never have met—community leaders, writers, musicians, or cultural icons—who have inspired and influenced us.

Offerings of Food

When humans gather to celebrate just about anything, there will be food. The custom of bonding through the sharing of food is universal, so much so that we continue to share food with people even after they have died. The practice of leaving food offerings for the deceased spans the globe, and it has been practiced throughout time. Traces of food offerings have been found among the grave goods of diverse cultures, from the tombs of ancient Egypt to the graves of Neolithic European farmers and within the burials of pre-colonial Indigenous North American peoples. It is such a part of the human experience to eat and share food that this impulse transcends life. Humans continue to hold on to food as a means to connect to those we love and respect, and we will lovingly provide this nourishment to those in the grave to ensure that they will not hunger in the afterlife. The act of eating gives us life, the act of sharing makes us

human, and providing food for the dead gives us hope for a life beyond this one.

Food for Grief

It can be hard to know what to do for someone who is grieving.
Words can be difficult to find in the presence of someone who has
just been hit with the loss of a loved one. This is an occasion when
actions really do speak louder than words, so showing up with a
lovingly prepared meal for the bereaved is a true act of thoughtful-
ness and concern. It is crucial for someone in the depths of grief to
eat healthy, nourishing food. This is a time when self-care tends to
be lost in the midst of managing all the emotions and shock of loss.
The bereaved may be struggling to figure out what their life will
be like now, planning a funeral, negotiating through complicated
legal matters, or dealing with financial upheaval in the wake of their
loved one's death.

Food can bring us comfort. A warm, easy-to-heat-up-and-serve
casserole or pot of homemade soup is a simple, kind, and thoughtful
way to care for someone who is grieving. You are not merely feeding
their body; you are also nourishing their spirit with the knowledge
that they have a friend who cares for them and wants them to be
comfortable and well fed. While casseroles are a traditional type of
dish for these circumstances, remember that breakfast, lunch, and
snacks will also be required. As tempting as sugary treats may be to
offer, healthy foods will provide better fuel for these difficult days.
A basket of fruit, some nice cheese, or some mixed nuts are easy to
graze on and will provide the antioxidants, minerals, and vitamins
that are needed to reduce stress and anxiety.

Samhain Season Food

Certain foods have an association with this time of year. Most of
these are late-harvest crops—the hearty, long-lasting, and easy-to-
store fruit and vegetables of the late autumn. The most iconic of
these is the pumpkin, not just for making jack-o'-lanterns, but also

for pies, quick breads, muffins, soups, and tasty curries. Long before pumpkins found their way from the New World to the Old, it was custom in Ireland to carve turnips with scary faces instead, believing that these creepy root vegetables would scare away any evil spirits that might be out for a lurk.

Apples are another popular Samhaintide treat and are a traditional handout for trick-or-treaters. Apple cider, apple pie, or any number of spiced, caramel-covered, or baked apple delicacies are very popular at this time of year.

An array of earthy-coloured rustic winter squash becomes available in time for Samhain, bearing evocative names such as buttercup, acorn, kabocha, honeynut, and delicata. Not only do they taste wonderful when simply roasted with a bit of butter, salt, and pepper, their autumnal colours and wonky shapes make them excellent seasonal decorations.

Dating back to at least the Middle Ages in Ireland and Britain, the tradition of making soul cakes became a popular way to celebrate Samhain, All Saint's Day (November 1), and All Soul's Day (November 2). These small, round, scone-like cakes usually contained dried fruit and nuts and were made to be handed out to children and beggars, who would go door to door, singing and praying for the souls of the dead. Soul cakes would often feature an equal-armed cross, either cut into the top or formed with raisins. This custom, a precursor to modern-day trick-or-treating, included a traditional rhyme (Broadwood and Maitland 1893, 31).

> *A soul! a soul! a soul-cake!*
> *Please good Missis, a soul-cake!*
> *An apple, a pear, a plum, or a cherry,*
> *Any good thing to make us all merry.*
> *One for Peter, two for Paul*
> *Three for Him who made us all.*

Tree nuts, such as chestnuts and hazelnuts, are also in abundance at this time of year, and October 31 is sometimes referred to as *Nutcrack Night*, when nuts would be used for various forms of divination. The English poet John Gay wrote of one method using hazelnuts. Two hazelnuts would be placed near a fire, representing a pair of sweethearts. If the nuts burned together, the pair would marry. If the nuts popped and jumped apart, it wasn't a match (1854, 55). Roasted nuts or baked goods made of nut flour are perfect food for a chilly fall night.

Raisin the Dead

When I think of what Samhain means to me, my mind wanders back to childhood and memories of Halloween trick-or-treating. Dressed in a festive costume, often covered by a parka if the weather didn't cooperate, I, along with countless other children, would scamper from door to door, on the hunt for candy and treats. The ultimate prize was a full-sized chocolate bar, and the booby prize was the dreaded box of raisins. As a kid, this felt like some kind of trick played on us by the grown-ups.

Raisins are the perfect food for celebrating the Samhain season. When I view them through the lens of my witchcraft, I see them as the last sigh of summer. Once a ripe and juicy grape, glowing and filled with sweet or tart refreshing goodness, the raisin is what is left when the summer has gone. Traditionally, raisins were left to wither and dry naturally either in the sun or shade. This slow process has been replaced by the use of dehydrators that can more efficiently reduce the grapes from about 80 percent water down to around 15 percent water. The final product is a darker, stickier, and sweeter version of its original form. In this state, our once-grape-now-raisin can be stored for the long winter, on hand when there is need for something sweet to be quickly prepared and shared.

In Mennonite and Amish communities, the humble raisin has been a staple ingredient in an understated and often overlooked delicacy: raisin pie. This dish, also called *Funeral Pie*, is such a staple at funeral feasts that mentioning it can be a foreboding omen. To say that "There will be raisin pie soon" means that someone is dying and there will be need for food to be prepared. In the days before raisins without seeds were available, in order to make a raisin pie, someone would need to deseed each small raisin by hand. The result would be worth it, as no matter the season, raisins could provide a sweet and delicious fruit pie to comfort those gathered for the funeral. Today, we have a wide variety of raisins to choose from: Thompson, sultana, golden, green, or red—all finding their way into our pantries without seeds, so no need to hand-pick them out anymore. Any type of raisin you may have on hand can be used for pie making.

I was introduced to raisin pie at a Finnish restaurant in Thunder Bay, Ontario. I was served a slice for dessert after a hearty meal along with a cup of coffee. It was intensely satisfying, and I was struck by the comforting simplicity of it—not too sweet, encased in a flaky pastry with no other embellishment. It was late September, and the food fit the season. I became obsessed with learning how to make this pie at home.

Over the years, I perfected my own recipe, adding spices and a generous amount of kitchen witchery into the mix. The raisins take me back to childhood trick-or-treating and to that dark time of year when the spirits of the dead walk alongside the living. Raisin Pie became Samhain Pie. The filling, as inky and dark as the underworld, is loaded with plump, succulent raisins, swelling with tasty sweetness. A reminder that even in the dark, there is a note of something sweet, a kind reminder as the darkening days draw the spirits closer and the wheel of death, rebirth, and life turns again.

References

Broadwood, Lucy E., and J. A. Fuller Maitland. *English County Songs*. Leadenhall Press, 1893.

Gay, John. *The Poetical Works of John Gay*. Vol. 2. Little, Brown, and Company, 1854.

"Nut-Crack Night." *Untold Lives* (blog). British Library. October 31, 2015. https://blogs.bl.uk/untoldlives/2015/10/nut-crack-night .html.

Cosmic Sway

Michael Herkes

As the leaves start to turn and the air gets crisp, there's a special kind of magic that seems to settle over the world. For those of us who follow earth-based spiritual paths, the end of the year is a time of profound transformation and powerful energy. From Halloween to the winter holidays, there's just something about this time that feels…different. Maybe it's the changing seasons, or maybe it's something more cosmic.

Observing Samhain

Samhain kicks off the Wheel of the Year on October 31. Observed by many as Halloween, it is more than a time of tricks and treats. Samhain is a time when many believe the veil between worlds grows thin, making it easier to connect with spirits, ancestors, and the otherworldly. Falling mid-Scorpio season, astrologically this further emphasizes the energy of transformation, emotional depth, and mystery. It's like the universe is giving us a cosmic nudge to look inward, face our shadows, and embrace change. It's a perfect moment to let go of what no longer serves us and set intentions for the year ahead.

One of the most significant ways to honor the spirit of Samhain is by creating an ancestor altar. Gather photographs, heirlooms, and mementos of your deceased family members, friends, or beloved pets. Arrange them on a table or in a special space in your home, and include candles to light in their memory. As you light each candle, take a moment to call out their names and express gratitude for their impact on your life. This altar can serve as a focal point for your Samhain celebrations, allowing you to reflect on your connections to those who have passed. You might also want to spend quiet time near the altar, journaling about your experiences or any messages you receive during this reflective period.

Candles are also essential for creating a warm and inviting atmosphere. Consider placing them in lanterns or hollowed-out pumpkins to enhance the magical ambiance. You can even create a small altar with seasonal items like crystals, dried herbs, and representations of the elements to honor the natural world.

Samhain is considered an auspicious time for divination, as the veil between the worlds is believed to be at its thinnest. Use this opportunity to seek insights into your future or connect with your intuition. You might try tarot readings or scrying with a crystal ball or black mirror for insight. Set aside time for a divination session, either alone or with friends. Share your findings and discuss what they might mean for your personal journey or collective experiences.

For those who wish to embrace the playful spirit of Halloween, this is a great time to craft your own Samhain-themed costumes or masks. This can be a fun way to connect with friends or family while celebrating the season. Consider using natural materials, like leaves or twigs, to create unique designs that reflect the essence of the season. Alternatively, host a costume party where everyone dresses up in their favorite witchy attire or as their favorite mythical creature. Encourage guests to share the stories behind their costumes, fostering a sense of community and creativity.

Full Moon in Taurus

As we move into November, we're greeted by a Full Moon in Taurus on November 5 at 8:19 a.m. Now, Taurus energy is all about grounding, comfort, and appreciating the physical world around us. It's like a cosmic hug after the intensity of Samhain. Taurus is a sign that is ruled by Venus, making this Full Moon an opportune time to focus on self-care, connect with nature, or do some rituals around abundance and beauty. You might want to take a luxurious bath mixed with rose petals and sensual sandalwood and vanilla oils, indulge in a decadent meal, or spend some time in a garden or park to really soak in the earthy Taurus vibes.

Mercury and Jupiter Retrogrades

Mid-November brings some interesting planetary shifts with Mercury going retrograde on November 9 at 2:02 p.m. and Jupiter following suit on November 11 at 11:41 a.m. Now, I know some get a bit nervous about retrogrades, especially Mercury's, but these can actually be really useful periods for reflection and inner work.

During Mercury retrograde, which lasts until November 29 at 12:38 p.m., you might find it helpful to revisit old projects, journal about past experiences, or focus on improving communication in your relationships. It's a great time for "re" activities: reviewing, revising, reconnecting.

Jupiter's retrograde, however, invites us to think about our personal growth and spiritual path. It's like the universe is asking us to pause our outward expansion for a moment and focus on internal growth. This could be a perfect time to deepen your meditation practice, explore new spiritual teachings, or reflect on your long-term goals and beliefs. This theme will carry on for a while, as Jupiter will remain retrograde until March 10, 2026, at 11:30 p.m.

Witchy Gratitude

As we approach the end of November, many people are celebrating Thanksgiving on November 27. Even if this isn't a holiday you typically observe, it can be a beautiful time to focus on gratitude and abundance. The Moon will be a waxing crescent in Aquarius then, which is a perfect time to focus on group activities since Aquarian energy connects to community. In the Moon's waxing phase, now is a time to take action in terms of gratitude—paying it forward and giving thanks for your blessings to come. You might consider sharing a meal with loved ones and taking turns expressing what you are grateful for using future tense. Or maybe you'd prefer to tap into Aquarius's independent and rebellious qualities with a solitary practice, like lighting a white candle and giving thanks to the universe, spirit guides, deities, etc. for your future blessings.

December Moons

The beginning of December is graced with a Full Moon in Gemini on December 4 at 6:14 p.m. Gemini energy is all about communication, learning, and connecting with others. This could be a great time to further expand on the energy from Thanksgiving by celebrating with a group ritual, sharing knowledge with fellow practitioners, or exploring new magical techniques. You might feel drawn to write new spells, start a magical study group, or simply engage in lively discussions about spiritual topics now.

Then, on December 19 at 8:43 p.m., the Moon's phase turns to new in the sign of Sagittarius. This feels like the perfect cosmic setup for setting big, bold intentions for the future. Sagittarius energy is adventurous, optimistic, and focused on growth. It's like the universe is encouraging us to dream big and believe in the possibility of those dreams coming true. This could be an ideal time for manifestation rituals, vision boarding, or setting ambitious goals for the coming year.

During this entire period, from Halloween to mid-December, the key is to stay open to the energy around you. Pay attention to how you feel during these cosmic events. You might notice that certain practices feel more powerful or that you're drawn to different types of magic than usual. Trust your intuition and don't be afraid to experiment.

Summary

As we journey through this magical season, from the mystical energies of Samhain to the hopeful promise of the Sagittarius New Moon, we're reminded of the cyclical nature of life and the constant opportunities for growth and renewal. This time of year, with its thinning veils and introspective energies, offers us a unique chance to connect deeply with ourselves, our ancestors, and the natural world around us.

Whether you're celebrating with a coven or practicing solitary magic, know that you're part of a larger tapestry of witches and Pagans honoring these ancient traditions. As we close this magical chapter and look toward the winter solstice, may you find peace in the darkness, strength in your spiritual practice, and hope for the light to come.

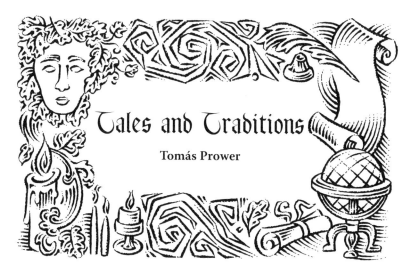

Tales and Traditions

Tomás Prower

SAMHAIN IS STRONGLY ASSOCIATED with the dead. Cultures the world over often focus this time of year on gazing into the world beyond—the world where our ancestors and all who have walked this earth now reside, the world where we will all one day be. But such a focused gaze goes both ways. Those in the realm of the dead also focus on and attempt communication with us during this season. Folks often explain this mutual reaching out to one another by saying that now is when "the veil between the worlds is thin"; though I, in my iconoclastic way, would add an overlooked asterisk to that by saying veils, by their very nature, are always thin. The memento mori revelations we get from Samhain are valid every season because, as mortals, death is always by our side. We just don't tend to acknowledge her presence during the other times of year…unless her scythe strikes a loved one, and then we're forced to acknowledge her and just how thin the veil always is.

Santa Muerte: A Strange Silence

In Mexico and Mexican diasporic communities throughout the world, particularly in the Southwestern regions of the United States, there is a strong and growing devotion to a syncretized folk deity known as La Santa Muerte. At her most basic core, Santa Muerte (whose name translates to "Holy Death") is death personified as a female grim reaper. Not a ruler of the underworld nor a divinity with patronage over the souls of the dead and whatever happens in the hereafter, Santa Muerte is death itself, and devotion to her is becoming one of the fastest-growing spiritual movements throughout Latin America. However, much to the joy of tabloid journalists and their insatiable need to crank out shock content of and dubious truth, the devotees of La Santa Muerte are predominately among the most maligned people in all of "respectable" Mexican society: criminals, sex workers, queer folx (particularly trans folx), cartel members, and many of those who are barred from earning a living through traditional means.

Why, though? Why is Death herself so popular among people who are ostracized by society? News outlets and the yellow journalism of our era would say it's obvious: these "dregs" of society would naturally gravitate toward something so unwholesome and evil because they themselves are unwholesome and evil. The truth, however, can only be seen through the lens of compassion and a stoic understanding of our own mortality. When all the world around you in the *machista,* Catholic Mexican society in which you live tells you that God hates you because of who you are or what you do, then certainly you can't go to God for help. Rather, you seek out help from forces that are also maligned and, thus, can sympathize with you. The fear of death is primal, and it is even stronger than the fear of the poor, the outcasts, and even criminals. Her devotees believe she listens and hears their prayers because Death is also an outcast of society, a thing to never be acknowledged, mentioned, or, if at all possible, allowed to exist.

All this I know on a firsthand level. As a Spanish-speaking Latino devotee of La Santa Muerte, I've met and worshipped with these outcasts of society on a level deeper than most academic "outsiders" can reach. Additionally, I'm a licensed mortuary professional who has worked in funeral homes where the daily duties of corpse handling and grief consoling get you through your existential dread of death really quickly in order to function on a daily basis. I've written two Llewellyn-published books on the magical spirituality of these matters (*La Santa Muerte: Unearthing the Magic & Mysticism of Death* and *Morbid Magic: Death Spirituality and Culture from Around the World*, respectively), but for this article here in this almanac, one lesson known to devotees who consistently get their prayers answered by Santa Muerte, and one that often gets overlooked during Samhain, is that of silence.

Silence is scary. I'm not talking about quietness or stillness. I mean silence—the silence of the grave. Our modern world constantly bombards us with sounds. City life is full of them, and even in rural areas, we constantly inundate ourselves with television, music, social media, and more, all to avoid having to sit in silence with our own thoughts. Total silence is uncomfortable. If you've ever been near a corpse, even (though to a lesser degree) amid the pomp and circumstance of a funeral, it's the silence that is particularly unnerving. Being alive is filled with so many little subconsciously noticed sounds, but to see a human body in ultimate silence is so unnerving that it can even be traumatic to those so unfamiliar with pure, true silence.

But silence is necessary. When devotees pray to Santa Muerte, they understand that communication, like reaching across the veil, is a two-way street. In order to receive the inspiration or advice she gives, you must be silent because you can't hear if you're busy talking. You have to quiet your mind to silence, because just as detrimental as constant yapping is the constant chatter going on in your mind. You have to able to mentally "listen" if you are to hear the answer to your prayers. But this level of silence takes a great amount of faith, which is why most people who pray for things never have their prayers answered. They're too busy asking for answers, and they neither "hear" them coming nor notice that they came and went.

When you pray to Santa Muerte, you pray once because you have faith that she heard you and faith that she'll answer you. Like with supplication to any other divinity, to continue asking just demonstrates your lack of faith that she listened or that she'll answer. So don't distract yourself away from silence, for that is how you "hear" the Divine and the unseen. That is true faith. And during Samhain in particular, don't always try to reach out to the other side, but rather, be silent so that you can "hear" them reach out to you now and every other season until you "see" them again.

Feasts and Treats

Nathan M. Hall

EVERYONE THINKS OF SAMHAIN as a great time to honor their ancestors and beloved dead, and it is! But it's also a time that I honor family, both those who have passed as well as those who are still with us. It's a time for the living and the dead to come together and enjoy a meal as they may have done in the past. In that vein, these recipes are some of my favorite family-night kind. When I want to feel close to my loved ones in the flesh and across the veil, I make this meal, or a variation of it, which I know has nourished and sustained my ancestors for countless generations.

Salt-Crust Roast Chicken

Don't be frightened by the salt in this recipe. After you bake the chicken, the salt breaks off like a shell and you can dust any excess away very easily.

Prep time: 20 minutes
Cooking time: 45–60 minutes
Servings: 4–6

3–4-pound chicken, organic preferred
Olive oil
Fresh herbs (a few sprigs of thyme or rosemary are wonderful)

½ lemon

3-pound box crystal kosher salt (I recommend Diamond, as other
    brands are too salty for my taste)

1 cup water

Preheat an oven to 450°F.

While the oven is heating, remove the chicken from the refrigerator and all packaging. Set on a platter and use paper towels to dry off any excess moisture. Inspect the cavity of the chicken and remove any giblets that may be included. (You could save them for later use in a stock.)

Pour a generous splash of olive oil into your hands and rub all over the outside of the bird, coating in an even, thin layer. Take the herbs and half of a lemon and place inside the cavity.

With some butcher's twine, tie together the legs, crossing them over one another. Turn the wings behind the back of the bird so they're pinned in place.

Leave the chicken on the platter and allow it to come up to room temperature while waiting for the oven to reach the correct temperature.

Into an oven-safe, deep-well skillet, roasting pan, or Dutch oven, pour out the contents of the kosher salt box. Don't fret! While you'll be using all—or as much as possible—of the salt, it won't overpower the chicken.

Add about a cup of water and mix it around until you get the salt to a slightly moist but easily clumping consistency. We'll be packing this all around the chicken, creating the "crust" that will act as a sort of plaster to maintain moisture—almost like a chicken-shaped Dutch oven. When you squeeze the salt in your hand, it should easily hold its shape. If it doesn't, try adding a little bit of water a splash at a time. Too much water and it will slide off the chicken.

Transfer the chicken into the salt breast-side down and begin packing the wet salt mixture all around the bird. Remember, we want a layer of salt sticking to it. Turn it over and continue packing the salt mix on the top and sides, squeezing a layer onto the drumsticks.

Let it roast in the oven for 45–60 minutes, until a thermometer stuck into the thick part of the thigh measures 160°F. The target temperature for poultry is 165°F, but it will continue cooking when removed from the oven.

Remove from the oven and allow the chicken to rest for about 10 minutes. The salt will sometimes take on a golden color in the oven. After it has rested, you can take the back side of a chef's knife and gently tap on the salt crust. It should fall apart in large chunks and be easy to separate from the chicken. The skin should come off with it, leaving unbelievably soft and juicy meat that is perfectly seasoned.

Once most of the salt has been removed, place the chicken on a serving platter and carve as you normally would.

French Bistro Potatoes with Rosemary

This is a classic potato recipe that will leave your guests wishing you had doubled the portions.

Prep time: 10 minutes
Cooking time: 30 minutes
Servings: 4

2 tablespoons kosher salt, or more to taste
2–3 large russet potatoes or a small bag of baby potatoes (I prefer russet potatoes for this recipe, but if you use baby potatoes, you can skip the parboiling step)
1 small, yellow onion, cut in half and very thinly sliced
Finely chopped rosemary
Any good, high-temperature cooking oil, but peanut oil is preferred for flavor

Fill a 6-quart pot ⅔ full of water, adding a healthy amount of kosher salt, about 2 tablespoons or more. While the water warms up, peel the potatoes and put the skins in the compost. (Or coat them with a little olive oil and salt, and crisp them in the oven for a chip-like snack.) Cut the potatoes into large, relatively uniform cubes, about ¾ of an inch.

After, take a mandoline or very sharp chef's knife and thinly slice the yellow onion and chop the rosemary.

When the water begins to boil, gently drop all of the potatoes in and let boil for 2–3 minutes. Best to use a timer so they don't get too soft. Use a slotted spoon or a skimmer to gently remove the potatoes and place them in a colander so they continue to drip dry.

Meanwhile, warm up a skillet over medium-high heat, adding enough peanut or other cooking oil to the pan to coat the bottom with a little extra that can easily move around the hot pan. Gently but quickly place the potatoes into the skillet and sprinkle a generous pinch of salt over the top.

Be patient and let them sit for about 7–10 minutes. Eventually, the bottom will crisp up nicely, and they'll easily unstick from the pan with a soft touch of your spatula. Once you've gotten them all to release, move them around the pan a bit, getting them to flip over, and allow to brown again. They should start looking a light golden color, brown in spots. Turn the heat down to medium and add the onion on top of the potatoes. Let them cook like that for about 4 minutes, and then gently stir them in, cooking for about 4 more minutes.

When the onions have gone translucent, sprinkle in some of the chopped rosemary and swirl the pan around a few times, allowing the rosemary to settle in between the potatoes. Turn off the heat and transfer to a serving dish. *Et voilà!*

Home-Brewed Mead

A warning ahead of time: This recipe will take up to 6 weeks before it's ready, so plan ahead. This is also a very bare-bones recipe that I use as a good starting point. There are countless home brewers, and, much like witches, every home brewer has ten opinions on the right way to do anything! If you try this recipe out and decide you want to dig deeper, I promise there's a lifetime of learning and experimentation you can do. I will not get into measuring specific gravity for calculating alcohol content, nor will I get into racking (transferring your mead from one container to another in order to effectively remove dead yeast, and thus, off flavors). If you do decide to brew more in the future, adding in these other elements will be very beneficial to the flavor (and reputation!) of your meads, beers, ciders, or wines.

The intent for sharing this recipe is to show you how easy it can be to start your brewing adventures and give you enough mead to share with friends and family at your next sabbat.

Prep time: 20–30 minutes

Brewing time: 6 weeks

Servings: 16 8-ounce servings, or one wild night

1-gallon glass jug

Airlock and bung

Large funnel

Large spoon

Large pot able to hold more than a gallon; 8 quarts should be adequate

Iodine (BTF Iodophor is a good brand)

2½ pounds honey

1 gallon distilled or filtered water

1 packet champagne yeast

Yeast nutrients (you can find small packets on brewing retailer websites)

Start by cleaning and sanitizing all of your equipment (glass jug, airlock and bung, funnel, large spoon, and large pot) with hot, soapy water. Rinse well and then let sit in a solution of iodine and cool water at a ratio recommended on package directions. Use your sink if it's big enough or a large plastic bin for this step.

After about a minute in the solution, remove the pot and place it on the stove. Add the honey and a few cups of water, and slowly warm over low-medium heat. Stir with the large spoon until the honey warms enough to mix well with the water. Pour into the gallon jug and pour in the remaining water. Add in the yeast and a packet of yeast nutrients and swirl until well incorporated. Some mead makers will add nutrients on successive days to make sure the alcohol content is as high as possible. Follow the instructions on the package that it comes in.

At this point, you can place the bung and empty airlock in the top of the jug and store in a cool, dark place. The following day, open the airlock and add some filtered water just to the line on the side. This will make sure that no bad bacteria gets in but the mead will still be able to off-gas without breaking your bottle.

Let sit for a minimum of 30 days, but aim for 6 weeks, or more if desired. When you're ready to try it out, you'll see a lot of silt at the bottom of the jug, which I mentioned earlier. Ideally, you don't want any of that in the part you drink because it's basically yeast poop and doesn't taste awesome. If you've really been bit by the brewing bug and know that you're going to make more after this, you can rack your mead into a clean and disinfected second gallon jug. If this is a one-time deal for you, though, you can just gingerly pour it out into mason jars, swivel-top bottles, or whatever you have on hand to transport it to your table or other function.

Crafty Crafts

Raechel Henderson

SAMHAIN IS TRADITIONALLY A time of divination. This time of year is known to bring the dead and recently departed closer to the land of the living. Witches take advantage of that proximity to tap into the wisdom of their ancestors through various forms of divination. They ask questions about the future, love, and money. The divination can be in the form of reading tarot cards, candle gazing, the swing of the pendulum, or even Spiritualists' practices, such as using a Ouija board. One type of divination that has gained popularity over the past few decades is oracle decks. Like the tarot, oracle cards provide messages from the Divine or the universe through a visual medium. Consider creating your own personalized set of oracle cards to use this Samhain.

DIY Oracle Cards

Creating your own oracle cards can be a deeply meaningful experience. You will be tapping into your personal interpretations of symbols and themes to come up with a deck that speaks directly to your soul. This can be a transformative project, urging you to dig deep. The joy of having a personal oracle is that you get more consistently meaningful answers to your questions. And this way you aren't stuck with interpretations that might not ring true to you.

This craft will take a lot of your time and energy to make, as you are creating an oracle from scratch. I suggest you take all the time you need rather than rushing through it. Also, you don't have to stick to one creative session. As the days, weeks, and months go on, if you find another card that should be part of your deck, take the time to make it and insert it. If a certain card stops feeling meaningful or helpful, you can always remove it from the deck. This will be a living, evolving divination tool.

Materials
Index cards
Markers, crayons, or colored pencils
Stickers or art transfers
Scrapbooking materials
Magazines, old books, and other visual media
Optional: selenite

Tools
Notebook, or a few pieces of paper
Scissors
Glue
Reference books and the internet
> *Cost:* $0–$20
> *Time spent:* Anywhere from a couple of hours to two weeks

Instructions
Begin by gathering your materials and creating sacred space. This is going to be an exercise in imagination and intuition, so you want to set the stage at the beginning. Call upon whatever spirits, deities, and ancestors you work with to help guide you through the process.

The first part of this craft requires you to consider what symbols speak to you. These can be archetypes, animals, colors, and crystals, even psychological terms. You can even have a mixture of symbols and themes. Sit down with a notebook or several pieces of paper and freewrite about the symbols. Go through each symbol on your list and write down whatever meaning comes to mind related to it. Don't censor yourself. Spend as much time as you want on this part of the process. It will be the basis for the entire oracle set. Come up with between thirty-six and fifty-two different symbols. Once you have your brainstormed list, put it aside for a day or two. Let the ideas gel and take shape outside of your conscious mind. Coming up with your own meanings before you research them will allow you to tap into your intuition before being influenced by others' interpretations.

When you are ready, sit down with your list and some reference books, such as dream dictionaries, books with correspondences like crystal and herb guides, dictionaries, and the internet. Don't be afraid to cast your net wide. Use a web search engine to look up the magical or mystical properties of each symbol. Read at least three sources on each symbol or theme if you can so that you get a good range of opinions on what each means. As you go about this, some meanings will pop up over and over again. Highlight these as major themes for that symbol. This part of the process will take some time—from a half an hour to a couple of hours depending on how long your list is. You might also find yourself editing as you go on, either deleting or adding symbols. This is perfectly fine. And as you write all this down, mark those meanings that resonate with you. Remember, you are making a personal divination tool, and it is how you interpret the meanings of your cards that makes it unique.

When you have finished the definition phase of this project, you'll have made your own unique table of correspondences.

Now begins the creative part of the process. You will create a card for each symbol in your master list. Use an index card for each one, decorating the card with images you've cut from magazines or old books, drawing with markers and colored pens, and using art stencils or transfers to create an image that encapsulates the symbol to your satisfaction. Don't be afraid to make a couple different versions of the cards to get to one that you love. Create cards for each symbol on your list, leaving the backs blank.

Take all the time you need to create the cards. This is where all the work you did previously will come to the forefront as you incorporate not only the symbol but its meanings in the image. And if you aren't feeling particularly artistic, you can always just write the symbol with the list of meanings on the front of the card. This is your deck, and you want it to speak to you personally.

When you are finished creating your deck, you'll want to cleanse it before use. A piece of selenite is perfect for cleansing. Lay the deck out with the selenite on top or below it for at least an hour. You can also cleanse and charge it under the light of the full moon or by setting it out in the sunlight at noon on a Sunday, the day of new beginnings.

To use your cards, shuffle them while thinking about your question. After you have shuffled your cards, pull one to answer your query. You can also use the cards in spreads as you would with any other deck. The key to keep in mind is that these cards are best for open-ended questions rather than yes-or-no ones. Also, because this deck has been made to your own specifications, I don't recommend using it in readings for others. They'll have their own interpretations of what the cards mean that won't have anything to do with the meanings that you imbued into the cards in the first place.

Samhain Meditations

Elizabeth Barrette

SAMHAIN IS THE LAST of the autumn sabbats and the most intro-spective. The trees are letting go of their leaves. This time of the year deals in death more than life, but it also focuses on the afterlife. It invites us to think of what will happen after we die and make life choices that aim us toward happiness in the hereafter. It reminds us of impermanence and transformation. Many mantras are suited to this time. You can also explore mindfulness itself. Look within and see what you can learn.

Mantra Meditation

Mantra meditation is among the simplest techniques. It is highly portable because all you really need is a selection of mantras. It is also versatile, as you can memorize a set of mantras for different needs. These aspects make it good for beginners.

This meditation focuses your mind on a desired blessing. It con-centrates your energy, increases your self-knowledge, and improves your psychic awareness. Use it to raise your consciousness or work on emotional healing. It's ideal to open and balance your chakras, as there are mantras for each one.

A *mantra* is a syllable, word, or phrase that encapsulates a key idea. You repeat it as a focus while you meditate. Think of your brain as a data storage device: It cannot simultaneously retrieve and record, and usually it can retrieve only one thing at a time. So while running a mantra, it cannot also extrapolate awful possibilities or replay traumatic memories. A mantra occupies your mind in a way that promotes peace.

Pretty much anything could be used as a mantra, but many traditions have developed a set of popular ones. Before beginning your practice, browse through options and choose one or more to try. Pick something that feels meaningful to you at your current stage of development. Make sure you can pronounce it confidently. You can say it silently or aloud. For a favorite mantra, you might want to get a copy of it on a wall hanging or altar stone. If you can't find a standard one that you like, you could always make your own.

You can repeat your mantra as much or as little as you want. Just set it to the amount you want to meditate. Some people like to chant their mantra for a specific number of times, such as 108 in Asian traditions. In this case, they often use a mala or some other type of prayer beads to help keep track of repetitions. You can buy one from a metaphysical supplier or make your own for personal significance.

For mantra meditation, it is best to find a quiet place with no noisy interruptions and where you won't bother anyone. You can do it on the go if necessary, though, by chanting silently in your head.

Sit in a comfortable position and take a few deep breaths to calm yourself. Turn your attention to your breath. Set your intention for this meditation session. Begin chanting your mantra. Think deeply about what it means to you. Let it resonate within you as you chant, filling your whole being.

Some popular mantras include:

Aham Prema
"I am divine love."

"The circle is open but unbroken."

"Earth, air, fire, water, spirit."

Ehyeh Asher Ehyeh
"I Am That I Am."

"I am enough."

"I am open to the possibilities of the Universe."

"Let it go."

Om Mani Padme Hum
"The jewel in the heart of the lotus."

Om Shanti
"Let there be peace."

"Return, return, return."

Mindfulness Meditation

Mindfulness lies at the core of most meditative practices, so it is a good skill to learn for any type of meditation that you want to do. It can be more challenging than some other techniques though. Some people want to start with fundamental skills like this. Others find it too hard and prefer to begin with something easier.

Many tools have been invented to assist mindfulness. Traditional versions include things like a *shishi-odoshi*, or tipping bamboo fountain, whose change in sound reminds you to focus on the present moment if your thoughts have wandered. Wall hangings, artwork, or statuettes placed around your home may remind you to take note of different things. A seashell in your bathroom may prompt mindfulness of water, while a cornucopia in the kitchen prompts mindful eating. In modern times, there are dozens of mindfulness apps that offer you a focus, guidance, or simply a reminder to stop and think about what you are doing right now.

Consider the benefits of mindfulness. It stops the annoying chatter of the "monkey mind." This reduces stress, lowers heart rate and blood pressure, slows breathing, and relaxes muscles. It can ease anxiety and depression. It deepens understanding of the body, which can help with chronic pain. It reduces sleep disturbances and boosts immunity. Mindfulness strengthens connections and relationships. It promotes kindness and compassion for yourself and others.

For mindfulness meditation, choose a quiet and peaceful place where nothing will interrupt you. You may sit on the floor or in a chair. Some people like to set the tone with temple incense, a beeswax candle, or a vase of flowers; others find such things distracting. Set a time span for your meditation; beginners often start with five-minute sessions. Breathe slowly and deeply.

Bring your attention to the present moment. Imagine it as the center of an hourglass, the narrow point where the future flows through to become the past. Focus your awareness on the flow, the way time feels as it seems to pour into and through and out of the present. Then narrow your attention further, letting the future and past fade out of your awareness, so you focus only on being in the moment.

If other thoughts come up, acknowledge them without judgment. Then let them go. If your feelings intrude, acknowledge the sensations without criticism. Then set them aside. Be an impartial witness. By not reacting in the moment, you cultivate your calm. You can always attend to these things later if they are important. Usually they are not.

Search for a center of calm. Seek the peace within you. Let your thoughts gradually become still and fade away. Imagine dissolving the edges of your mind. Become one with the world around you, without judgment, without thought. There is only the here and now.

You can also watch for opportunities to practice mindfulness in everyday activities. In your morning and evening routines of self-care, choose to be good to yourself. When you eat, take time to savor the food. Before you pass through a door, note the transition. Walk mindfully and notice the world around you.

At the time of death and rebirth, think about how you can be aware of your soul's journey. Practices like mantras and mindfulness can help you frame your exeriences in the context of your life.

Samhain Ritual

Dodie Graham McKay

THIS RITUAL IS INTENDED to be shared with others. Just make sure that you prepare enough pie in advance so that there is a slice for everyone, plus one slice to set out as an offering to your beloved or mighty dead. This is an ideal activity for your coven or working group, but the folks you invite do not need to be witches or Pagans to participate. You may also perform this ritual alone, which means you will have leftover pie, and that is a very good thing!

Dessert with the Dead

I have adapted the traditional, basic way of making raisin pie, or Funeral Pie as it is known in Amish and Mennonite communities, to make it more fitting for my own Samhain celebrations by adding rum extract and spices. Some versions of Funeral Pie also include walnuts, but I am a raisin purist and prefer to leave out nuts. If you want to add some chopped walnuts to your pie, omit a half cup of the raisins and add a half cup of chopped walnuts when you stir in the butter, orange juice, and zest.

Preparing for the Ritual

The ritual begins for you when you set your intention to make the pie and hold the ceremony. You will be baking the pie not just as a dessert but as an offering to your guests and yourself. Bake it with the intention to celebrate the beloved and mighty dead who you have loved, admired, and learned from.

To prepare for this ritual, you will need to plan a few things in advance:

- Invite friends or family to a potluck dinner. Ask them to bring a food item that was a favourite of someone they were close to who has died.
- Ask each of your guests to bring a photo of a beloved or mighty dead that they want to tell a story about.
- Go grocery shopping for the ingredients you need to make Samhain Pie. As you are selecting your items, focus on the ritual you will be hosting and your intention to honour those who have died.

Baking the Pie

Gather together your ingredients and baking equipment, setting out everything you need within easy reach. Pause. Take three deep breaths and say:

I prepare this food with my hands, as my ancestors' hands have fed me.

I prepare this food with my mind, as my ancestors' minds have known me.

I prepare this food with my heart, as my ancestors' hearts have loved me.

As you handle each ingredient, focus on its colour, texture, and smell. Celebrate the joy that being alive and able to interact with the pleasures of these simple ingredients brings you. Some of the ingredients I have added for their magical associations:

- Rum extract to represent an offering of alcohol to the spirits of your beloved and mighty dead.
- Cinnamon to bring love and comfort as you remember your beloved and mighty dead.
- Nutmeg to boost your psychic connection to the spirit world.
- Allspice to aid in healing from the pain of loss.

You may choose to assign magical correspondences to the other ingredients in this recipe or to enjoy and celebrate them as foods of the earth working together to nurture and sustain the bodies of you and your guests.

Samhain Pie Recipe

The next step is to bake your pie. In addition to preparation and baking time, factor in cooling time for the pie; it will cut nicer and be easier to serve if it is at room temperature or chilled. Baking it the day before you intend to serve it works really well.

Prep time: 1 hour (This will vary depending on whether the pastry dough is homemade or store bought.)

Cooking time: 45 minutes

Servings: 8 (or 7 guests, plus 1 slice for the offering plate)

Pastry dough for a 9-inch, double-crust pie (store bought or homemade both work great)

3 cups raisins (sultanas or Thompsons are my favourites, but use what you have)

3 cups water

2 teaspoons rum extract

½ cup brown sugar, packed

3 tablespoons cornstarch

½ teaspoon cinnamon

⅛ teaspoon nutmeg

⅛ teaspoon ground allspice

¼ teaspoon salt

1½ tablespoons butter

1 tablespoon orange juice

Zest from 1 orange
1 egg yolk
1 tablespoon water

Chill dough in the refrigerator. Preheat oven to 425°F.

Add raisins, water, and rum extract to a saucepan and let soak for 30 minutes. In a bowl, mix together the brown sugar, cornstarch, cinnamon, nutmeg, allspice, and salt. Then put the saucepan with the raisins onto the stove and bring it to a gentle boil over medium-high heat. Stir the sugar and spice mixture into the saucepan with the raisins.

Continue cooking over medium heat and stir until the mixture becomes syrupy. Simmer gently, stirring often for about ten minutes. Remove from heat and stir in the butter, orange juice, and zest. Mix thoroughly. Let the mixture cool down while you prepare the crust.

Roll out half of your pastry dough and use it to line a 9-inch pie dish. Roll out the other half of your dough and set it aside. This will be your top crust.

Gently pour your raisin filling into the prepared pie dish, spreading it evenly. Gently cover with the top crust and then seal the edges by crimping the top and bottom crusts with your fingers. Cut some slits to allow steam to vent.

Beat the egg yolk with the water, ensuring that it is very well blended. Use a pastry brush to paint the top crust with a thin, even layer of the egg wash.

Bake in the middle of the oven for ten minutes, then reduce the temperature to 350°F for an additional 30–35 minutes. Remove from oven and let the pie cool down completely; use a wire rack if you have one.

The Ritual

Before your guests arrive, set up the ritual space. This will be the area where you and your guests will be sharing the potluck dinner. Set the table with your best dishes. If you have dishes you inherited from a family member, now is a good time to use them. Table linens or flatware that have been handed down through the generations would also enhance the intention. Add a vase of seasonal flowers, your favourite candlesticks—be as creative as you are able. Incorporate anything you have that speaks to you about your beloved and mighty dead. Involve as many senses as possible. Select background music that evokes fond memories and nostalgia. Do not forget that smell is one of the strongest triggers for memory: incense, an essential oil diffuser, or a fragrant simmer pot of herbs can offer scent that brings back connection to deceased loved ones.

Set up a simple altar on a side table, or, if your dining table is large enough, set your altar space in the middle of it. You will need enough space to hold a small bell, a black candle, a lighter or matches, the photos you and your guests will bring, the Samhain Pie, enough small plates and forks for each guest, a knife to cut the pie, and a spatula or lifter to serve it. Feel free to add any other seasonal decorations that you like.

When your guests arrive for the potluck, the ritual begins for them. Lay out your main potluck meal, and when everyone has been seated, start with a toast:

We gather tonight to honour our beloved and mighty dead.
We eat and drink to remember that we are alive, and so long as we remember those who have left us, they are never truly gone.
Hail the beloved and mighty dead!

Encourage your guests to fill their plates and enjoy the food. Remind them to savour the abundance of life and the gifts of food and friendship. Allow for plenty of time for everyone to eat their fill and enjoy the experience.

When the meal is done, clear up the dinner plates, turn off any music, and ask everyone to make sure their phones are on silent. Ask everyone to get their photos ready. Explain that this will be the part of the evening when each person will take a turn sharing a short story about their beloved or mighty dead and add their photo to the altar. Share some of the information you have learned from reading about the lore of Samhain Pie with them.

Once everyone is ready, ring the bell, then light the black candle. Starting with the person immediately to your left, invite them to tell their story, then add their photo to the altar. When they are done, instruct them to ring the bell and say, "[Name of dead person]. I name my dead!" Continue around the room until everyone has had a chance to add their story and photo.

After the last person has spoken, serve each person a slice of pie, and then cut an extra slice to leave on the altar as an offering to the beloved and mighty dead. Explain to your guests that you will be eating the pie in silence to allow for communion and connection with the spirits of deceased loved ones.

When the pie has been eaten, ring the bell again, thank the spirits and the guests for contributing to this great feast, and invite them to stay for whatever fun may follow.

On the following day, the piece of pie left as an offering can be buried outside, burned in a ritual fire if you have a safe way to do so, or wrapped reverently in a piece of biodegradable material and, with thanks, deposited in your garbage bin.

Notes

Notes

Yule

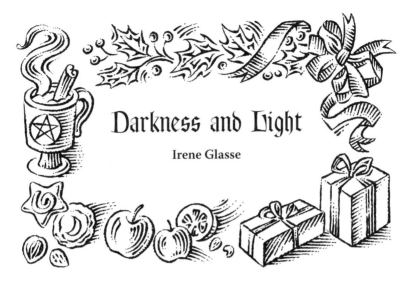

Darkness and Light

Irene Glasse

THE WORD *YULE* IS linguistically rooted in the cultures of the ancient Anglo-Saxons, Norse, and Proto-Germanic peoples. These lands where our earliest hint of Yuletide first arose are far north of the equator—climates that are not just dangerously cold in winter but also dark. They are regions where sunlight only shines for a few hours or less during the shortest days of the year. Winter in the far north was a harsh experience before the advent of electricity and other modern conveniences.

Imagine it for a moment: you and your family cluster around the fire in a small, dark dwelling. You can hear the soft sounds of livestock nearby. To survive winter, any animals you care for must also live indoors. The wind howls beyond the walls, shrieking through the snow-covered valleys and settlements, singing the song of winter into the long, dark nights. The tales associated with these deep, cold winters are bleak ones. The Wild Hunt rides the night: a spectral gathering of hounds, horses, and ghostly hunters seeking lost souls and anyone foolish enough to be out alone after the fall of darkness. The *draugar*, terrifying undead creatures from ancient Scandinavian folktales and sagas, are thought to be more active during the dead of winter. Trolls and *jötnar*, powerful beings associated with primal and sometimes destructive forces, are wandering the land. The weather is dangerous, but the folkloric beings active during the frigid darkness of winter are even more so. In the ancient world of the far north, deep winter was a time to grab your loved ones close and hold on tight.

The harshness of that ancient winter experience brings into focus how powerful the early celebration of Yule must have been. It was a shining source of connection, a celebration of the power of community, and a bright light of hope in the midst of dark, challenging days. The earliest festivities of Yule are attested to have included the swearing of solemn oaths, sacrifices, feasting, toasting, and the tending of large fires in the pre-Christian temples where Yule was being celebrated. Although the records of that time are incomplete, we can see tantalizing clues as to the importance of Yule: one of the names for Odin, the lead deity of the old Norse pantheon, is *Jólnir*, meaning "the Yule one."

It's easy to lose track of how sacred and vital pre-Christian Yule was underneath the onslaught of the modern winter holiday season. Despite the rush of activities and sensory overload of contemporary Yuletide, the profound nature of the earliest iterations of the holiday remains for those who seek it. It was an attempt to reshape my own experience of Yule that drew me to new traditions rooted in those earlier observances.

December is hard for me, you see. Over the years, an unusual number of my close friends and family members have died during the month of December, including my beloved father. The weight of grief and the parade of heartbreaking anniversaries began to be more than I could carry. As a child, I loved the winter holidays and was the kind of goofball who would wander around wearing a red-and-white Santa-style hat all month. In my younger years, I baked, decorated, threw holiday parties, and more, all with a good deal of festive cheer.

As much as I tried to maintain some sort of connection to the Yuletide traditions I'd previously engaged in, I found that my heart just wasn't in it. I felt like I was pressed against a window watching Yuletide arrive for others but unable to join in. The brash cheeriness and extroversion of the holiday season began to be something I dreaded. It felt like the explosion of color and brightness only served to highlight my pain.

After a few years of difficult Decembers, I decided to try a new approach more deeply rooted in the pre-Christian celebrations of the holiday in the hope that it would help me connect to the sacred season in a healthier way.

One thing my students most likely get tired of me saying is, "The power of aesthetics cannot be underestimated." I truly believe in the power of symbolism and the impact of color, shape, and form on the mind. To reshape my Yuletide, I began with a symbol shift. My previous Yuletide decorating scheme leaned strongly toward black, silver, and purple ornaments, garlands, lights, and wreaths. Although those colors are beautiful, that set of decorations lived through the hard years with me, and it was time to let them rest. I elected to keep that entire set with the thought that in future years I might be able to bring it out once more or pass it on to someone who needs it.

To connect more intentionally with the solar aspects of the holiday, I began to gather gold ornaments of various sorts. I asked friends to keep me in mind as they broke out their holiday collections, and if they had any used and unwanted gold ornaments to pass them along. I also started regularly checking resale, thrift, and consignment shops for collections of inexpensive solar-colored decorations. I bought a few strings of warm white twinkle lights as well as two strings of yellow lights.

My home slowly filled with the warm glow of flame-colored lights, shining gold ornaments, sun symbols, and more. I bought a new wreath for the door from a local craft store and painted symbols on the faux gold apples of the wreath to invite winter blessings. In the evenings after dinner, I lowered the lights and allowed the warm glow of twinkle lights and candlelight to fill my home. I began to feel more connected to the cycle of the sun and my own position in the Wheel of the Year.

Along with intentionally shifting my Yuletide aesthetics, I committed to a spiritual practice that I'd heard of but had not yet tried: Sunwait.

Sunwait: A New Tradition

Sunwait, or *Väntljusstaken,* is a contemporary candle-lighting practice that originated in Sweden and was intentionally designed to offer an experience similar to the Christian tradition of Advent. Sunwait begins six weeks before the winter solstice and is a beautiful way to focus on the meaning of waiting for the light within the darkness.

To celebrate Sunwait, adherents gather six candles together. One candle is lit per week leading up to Yule, most frequently at sunset, and the meaning of that candle and the promise of the return of the sun is focused on. After a time of connection and contemplation, the candle is snuffed. As the weeks pass, each previously lit candle is kindled along with the new candle for that week. The day of the week for lighting each candle is adaptable—some people light the next candle on a Thursday, some on a Sunday, some on the day of the week the winter solstice falls on that year, and some simply when it best fits their schedule. Some people light their candle(s) every night, others only on the evening they have selected for adding the next candle. Additionally, each candle is associated with a rune—a symbol from the Elder Futhark, one of the alphabets used in contemporary Heathen practice as both a written language and a magical sigil system. In the Elder Futhark, each rune has a meaning as well as a letter it represents. Some families include the reading of rune poems—poems that offer an explanatory poetic stanza for each rune they've chosen. There are also stanzas specific to Sunwait that can be found on websites and forums dedicated to the practice.

Although there are commonly used runes for each candle, the choice of rune or sigil is also fully adaptable. In my own family's practice, we selected runes that represented qualities we wished to bring into our lives in the coming year. Sunwait can be further adapted to include symbols and sigils other than runes.

Selecting and preparing Sunwait candles can be a meaningful experience for the household. Any six candles can be used, and if you are unable to have open flame in your home, battery-powered candles work just as well as traditional ones. Candles can be any shape, size, or color, and both the candles and the candleholders you decide to use can be decorated.

Carve, draw, or paint the rune, symbol, or sigil you've chosen for each candle onto the candle or candleholder for each day of Sunwait. You can deepen the practice further by anointing the candle with an appropriate oil, charging it with the energy of your selected symbol, or adding more decorations. Then, place your Sunwait candles in their holders on your altar or wherever you plan to honor Sunwait. My family placed our Sunwait candles on the dining room table.

We chose large gold pillar candles for our Sunwait practice and placed them on a metal tray with a protective lip along with natural objects from the land where we live: pine cones, small boughs from the pine trees, and a few fallen leaves. It worked best for our schedule to celebrate Sunwait on Sundays, so at sunset on the five Sundays leading up to the winter solstice, we lit the appropriate candle and meditated on the meaning of the rune we'd selected. We allowed a half hour or so for contemplation, connection, and welcoming the light of the candle(s) into our home, then snuffed the candle(s). Then, on Yule, we lit the last candle at sundown. Seeing the slow spread of light from one lit candle all the way to six lit candles over that six-week period was a beautiful foreshadowing of the growing sunlight to come.

Since my household selected larger candles, we were able to expand the practice further. We eat dinner together, so we relit our Sunwait candle(s) when we ate our evening meal and dimmed the overhead lights. The combination of candlelight and the presence of the symbol(s) on the lit candle(s) added a layer of connection to our daily lives that was truly beautiful. Additionally, we continued to light the candles after Yuletide passed, allowing them to slowly burn down over the course of each dinner together. The last candle finally burned out, appropriately enough, just before the vernal equinox. With this more extended expression of Sunwait, we invited the light of Yule to truly fill the darkest months.

Practicing Sunwait can be as complex or simple as fits your needs. It is a new tradition with very general guidelines, so it is fully open to interpretation and customization.

The Light That Lingers

Intentionally shifting the focus of Yuletide toward the cycle of the sun dramatically changed my experience of the entire Yuletide season. I began to feel more connected—to the intertwining of darkness and light, the incredible power of symbols of hope and resilience amidst winter's cold, and the thread leading back thousands of years to the ancestors of contemporary Heathen and Pagan beliefs. I could sense the resonance of the holiday again, the potent power of coming together to celebrate not despite the cold and darkness but *because* of it. I remembered anew that Yule is also a story of resilience and the seasonal lesson that light returns, no matter how dark the night.

My grief was still present, but the edges weren't as sharp. I had my first "good" December in five years. There were tough days but also moments of beauty, joy, depth, and connection. I am learning new approaches to enjoying Yule. Choosing to reach more deeply into the history of the holiday changed Yuletide for me in beautiful ways.

Transformation is the gift of magickal practice, and we have no greater example of powerful transformation than the winter solstice's shift from darkness to light. If Yuletide has become a challenging holiday for you, I hope you'll consider some transformation of your own: change the symbols, add a new practice, allow yourself grace, and see what the growing light reveals.

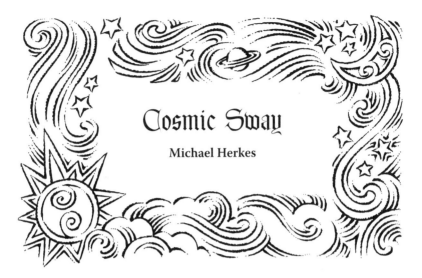

Cosmic Sway

Michael Herkes

As the Wheel of the Year turns, we find ourselves approaching a time of profound change and renewal. Welcome to the Yuletide season, a time when many may feel a special pull toward reflection and magical practice. This period between Yule and the next sabbat blends the introspective energy of Capricorn with the heart-centered lunar creativity of Leo, offering a unique atmosphere for personal growth and celebration.

Observing Yule

The Winter Solstice, or Yule, marks the longest night of the year. It's a moment when many pause to honor the return of the Sun and the gradual lengthening of days. Some folks celebrate by lighting candles or burning a Yule log, symbolizing hope and the promise of spring to come. This time also kicks off Capricorn season, which brings a grounded energy that's great for setting long-term goals and committing to your spiritual path.

It's interesting to note how many Christmas traditions have roots in older, Pagan practices. The use of evergreens, mistletoe, and gift-giving all harken back to ancient winter celebrations.

Whether you celebrate Christmas or not, this time of year can be a wonderful opportunity to express gratitude and focus on renewal.

Here's a simple ritual I crafted based on Fiona Horne's Pentagram Salute (Horne 2000, 132). You can perform this rite at sunrise on Yule to welcome the return of the Sun. Find a spot outdoors where you can see the eastern horizon. Alternatively, do this from a window inside your home that faces east. Bring a candle, matches or lighter, and any other items you wish to have with you. Light the candle and ground and center yourself. Take a few deep breaths and feel your connection to the earth beneath you. Face east and raise your arms in greeting as the Sun begins to rise. Perform the pentagram salute:

- Touch your forehead and say, "Blessed be my mind."
- Touch your right chest and say, "Blessed be my heart."
- Touch your left shoulder and say, "Blessed be my body."
- Touch your right shoulder and say, "Blessed be my soul."
- Touch your left chest and say, "Blessed be my power."
- Touch your forehead and say, "Blessed be the returning light."

As the Sun rises, visualize its warm, golden light filling you with renewed energy and hope. Spend a few moments in quiet reflection or meditation. Thank the Sun and any deities or spirits you've called upon. Ground excess energy into the earth and extinguish your candle.

New Year's Magic

As we move into the new year, many people feel a natural urge to set intentions and make fresh starts. For those who practice magic, this can be a powerful time for cleansing rituals and spellwork focused on manifesting desires for the coming year. The concept of New Year's resolutions can be done with a magical twist. On the night of New Year's Eve, light a white candle and ground and center your energy. Shuffle a deck of tarot cards and pull one card for each of the twelve months ahead: January 2026–December 2026. Reflect on each of the cards and their associated energy that corresponds to that month. On a piece of paper, write out an affirmation or resolution that aligns with the energy of each card. Then, at the stroke of midnight, burn your paper safely in a fireproof bowl or cauldron and allow the flames of transformation to send your resolutions into the universe.

New Year Moons

The first Full Moon of 2026 falls in Cancer on January 3. Cancer energy is all about emotions, home, and nurturing, making this a great time for self-care and emotional healing. You might feel drawn to spend time at home, connect with family, or do some divination work. It's a good moment to check in with your feelings and set intentions for emotional well-being in the year ahead.

Later in the month, on January 18, we have a New Moon in Capricorn. This is an excellent time for setting serious, long-term goals. New Moons are a time to plant the seeds of your intentions, and Capricorn energy is all about discipline and hard work, so any intentions you set now have a good chance of manifesting if you put in the effort. Now is a great time to wear crystals like garnet or onyx to enhance focus and determination while aligning with Cap energy.

Finally, we round out this lunar period with a Full Moon in Leo on February 1. Leo energy is bold, creative, and confident. This Moon encourages us to step into our power, express ourselves authentically, and celebrate our unique gifts. It's a wonderful time for creative projects, self-love rituals, or anything that allows you to shine your light brightly.

Throughout this whole period, from Yule to the Leo Full Moon, there's a beautiful progression of energy. We start with the quiet introspection of winter, move through the grounded goal-setting of Capricorn season, and end with the fiery self-expression of Leo. It's like a journey from the depths of winter to the first stirrings of spring.

Each of these Moon phases offers unique opportunities. As we move into Cancer's emotional waters, healing and nurturing spells could be powerful. During the introspective Capricorn period, you might focus on banishing rituals to clear away what no longer serves you. And when Leo's lunar energy arrives, it's a perfect time for confidence-boosting and creative magic.

Remember, though, that these are just suggestions based on astrological events. The most important thing is to listen to your own intuition and do what feels right for you. Magic is deeply personal, and what works for one person might not resonate with another.

Summary

As we conclude our journey through this magical Yuletide season, from the depths of the winter solstice to the fiery creativity of the Leo Full Moon, we're reminded of the cyclical nature of life and the constant opportunities for growth and renewal. This time of year, with its introspective energies and promise of returning light, offers us a unique chance to connect deeply with ourselves, our goals, and the natural world around us.

The rituals and practices we've explored—from honoring the solstice to harnessing the power of the Full and New Moons—are more than just traditions. They're powerful tools for self-discovery, healing, and manifestation. As we engage in these practices, we align ourselves with the rhythms of nature and the cosmos, tapping into energies far greater than ourselves.

Reference

Horne, Fiona. *Witch: A Magickal Journey: A Hip Guide to Modern Witchcraft*. Thorsons, 2000.

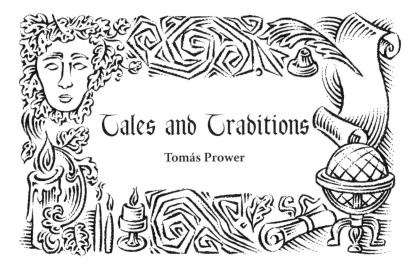

Tales and Traditions

Tomás Prower

YULE IS A SEASON of extremes: polar opposites existing together in contradiction to each other, which paradoxically amplifies their differences and reveals how they are linked—opposite sides of the same coin, two halves of a whole. Most notably, this is seen during Christmas and the winter holidays across the world, wherein merriment, joy, and light are amped up to artificial excess during a time when nature and the earth are filled with maximum solitude, stillness, and darkness. Compared to all the other sabbats, Yule has proven the world over that we humans can make the best out of a bad situation and still find reasons to celebrate amid difficult times, because neither the light nor the dark can exist without one another.

The Aurora: Lights in the Darkness

The Inuit peoples of North America, whose cultures have adapted to the Arctic Circle, experience the extremes of light and dark in a way rarely seen outside earth's polar regions. Because the earth's vertical axis is at an angle, during Yule, the Northern Hemisphere tilts back away from the sun, creating the effect of even shorter days and longer nights the closer one gets to the North Pole. Known as the "Land of the Midnight Sun," this is very apt for summertime, but here in winter, the opposite is true—a "Land of the Midday Moon," so to say. During this time of Yule, the longest night of the year gets exaggerated in the Arctic due to the positioning of the earth at this point of the solar cycle.

This extended darkness allows for more opportunity to see one of the most spectacular phenomena: the aurora borealis. Literal lights in the darkness, auroras are caused by streams of charged particles from the sun (known as *solar flares*) interacting with and disrupting the earth's magnetosphere, resulting in dazzling curtains of ghostly light ranging from shades of red and green to blue and purple. And though auroras are most active during the equinoxes, it's during Yule when they are most visible. The ability to see them is a gift of the season's pronounced darkness.

To the native peoples of the Arctic regions of North America, the aurora borealis was often interpreted as the ancestors attempting to get in touch with us in the living world. Though some Inuit cultures saw the phenomenon as an omen of ill, to other cultures, these dancing lights were seen as a window into the afterlife, showing the brightness, joy, and Technicolor merriment in which their ancestors were reveling. This interpretation closely matches our own Westernized interactions with Yule: holiday parties of togetherness, merriment, and strings of multicolored blinking lights adorning our surroundings.

In both cases, it's the darkness of the season that makes these lights special. The aurora occurs all year long, not only during the lower depths of winter. And parties with garish lighting take place every month of the year, not just December. Still, it's because of the winter darkness that the aurora—that window into another world where all is merry and bright—is most vibrantly seen and witnessed. It's because of the winter darkness that Christmas, Hanukkah, Kwanzaa, and other Yule-time parties of togetherness amid electric lights of splendor feel a little more magical.

Sure, the aurora can be seen during Litha, but it won't be as spectacular. And twinkling Christmas lights can be used during a summer get-together, but they don't seem to have the same magic. Opposites the world over complement one another. It's because of the depths and lengths of darkness during Yule that certain Inuit cultures get their strongest glimpse into the bright world beyond, and it's because of that same cold darkness that allows the multicolored lights and candles of winter holidays to stand out and shine. The extremes of life, paradoxically, always allow their opposite their strongest time to be noticed and appreciated.

Sedna: Power from the Abyss

The Inuit goddess Sedna is an example of this paradox—a mythological expression of the Yule-appropriate maxim "It's always darkest before the dawn." In this case, the darkest moment of one goddess turned into the beginning moment of her greatest power. Specifics about the legend vary upon tribe and oral tradition, but at its most generalized core, this particular legend about Sedna revolves around her tempestuous relationship with her father, the creator deity Anguta.

According to one version of the legend, Anguta is unhappy with his daughter's unwillingness to be married. More than just being uninterested in all the male suitors who come courting, Sedna is uninterested in the concept of marriage as a whole and the ties that bind each spouse to the other. After shaming her father by jokingly marrying a dog to show her loathing for marriage, her father decides to get rid of her by dumping her into the middle of the sea and cutting off her fingers to ensure she could not get back into the boat to further shame him with her intense sense of independence.

This was the darkest moment for Sedna. Betrayed by the very person who should have unconditionally loved and protected her, it was he who proved most intolerant and dangerous toward her. Now, stuck at the bottom of the sea, this would have been the tragic end for Sedna, but it was just the beginning of her greatest happiness. For, you see, down in the dark depths of the sea, Sedna found a female companion whom she loved and who loved her in equal measure. Also, with the sea being her new domain, she utilized it to become one of the most powerful deities among the pantheons of the Inuit peoples. The bounty of the sea was the main food source for many Inuit peoples, and as now-ruler of the sea, Sedna held the power of life and death over humanity by being able to give and withhold from them their main food source.

And so it is with us today. Like the aurora, the darkest time of year allows the brilliance of light to be at its most visible. Like Sedna, the darkest times in our lives can be the impetus and beginning point for the greatest times in our lives. Yule is the time to be aware of and celebrate this. Celebrate the darkness's ability to emphasize light and celebrate endings for the new beginnings they bring.

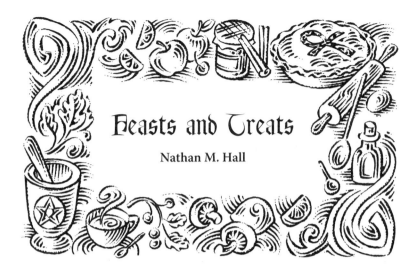

Feasts and Treats

Nathan M. Hall

When I think of Yule, I reflect on the light returning and the days growing longer, as well as a little bit of hope, for my family and for my community, that everything is in the hands of the goddess.

Vegetarian Mushroom Wellington

I created this recipe when I was still an active vegetarian. While it's been some years since then, it holds up well even for those who are more carnivorous.

Prep time: 25 minutes
Cooking time: 45 minutes
Resting time: 10 minutes
Servings: 6–8

1 box puff pastry (Substitute vegan puff pastry if desired; grab a second box if you'd like to make decorations.)
Olive oil
1 large red onion, peeled, cut in half, and sliced thin
Kosher salt
32-ounce baby bella, cremini, or white button mushrooms (about 4 of the small cartons or 2 larger cartons that you find in the

grocery store), rinsed well and sliced, removing any stems that are too tough

1 shallot bulb, peeled and very thinly sliced

5 cloves garlic, peeled and minced

6 ounces chopped walnuts

1½ tablespoons Worcestershire sauce (Substitute soy sauce if you don't want the anchovy)

½ cup red wine

Fresh rosemary, chopped well

Fresh ground black pepper

Egg wash (1 egg mixed with a couple tablespoons of water).

The night before you need it, move the puff pastry from the freezer to the refrigerator. If you're short on time, you can thaw it on the countertop in about an hour.

Preheat your oven to 400°F.

Put a large saucepan over low-medium heat and add enough olive oil to evenly coat the bottom in a thin layer once the pan has warmed up. Add thinly sliced red onions to the pan and put a healthy pinch of kosher salt over the top. Stir briefly and begin to allow the onions to caramelize. Stir occasionally for the next 10–15 minutes.

Once the onion has begun to be a bit translucent, add in the sliced mushrooms and increase heat to medium or medium-high. Add a pinch more salt and sweat the mushrooms, evaporating out most of the liquid that is expressed as they cook.

While the pan still has some of the mushroom liquid in it, add in the shallot and minced garlic and allow to cook until very fragrant. Add in chopped walnuts and immediately follow with the Worcestershire sauce and the red wine. Allow to simmer until the alcohol reduces, most of the liquid has been absorbed, and the walnuts have softened. If necessary, add in ½ cup water to further help the walnuts soften. Add the rosemary, black pepper, and more salt to taste and remove from heat.

On a sheet of parchment paper, dust a few pinches of flour down, unfold the puff pastry, and roll it out with a rolling pin to increase the area of the dough by a few inches. Brush on a thin layer of egg wash across the entire exposed dough. Take the mushroom filling and spoon it lengthwise down the center of the pastry dough. The filling should form a nice even layer, about 3 inches wide, that you can form with your hands to stand up a couple inches. Gently fold over one side of the dough to just cover the mix and brush that layer with more egg wash. Fold over the other layer and stretch just slightly to completely cover the first. Press the two layers together. Pinch to seal each open end and then carefully tuck under. Brush on one final layer of egg wash. Slice a couple small vent holes through the top.

If you want to get fancy, you can add some decorations made from another roll of puff pastry. Leaf patterns, mushrooms, stars, or even lattice patterns are all appropriate and will give your guests a little extra surprise. Just cut out the shapes freehand with a small paring knife and brush the Wellington loaf with egg wash, placing the patterns on top, and then put another layer of egg wash over them.

Transfer the parchment paper to a sheet pan and bake until the pastry is a beautiful golden brown, about 45 minutes. Pull the Wellington out of the oven and let rest for about 10 minutes before transferring to a serving platter.

Roasted Root Vegetables

These are a good pairing with the Vegetarian Mushroom Wellington because they can occupy the oven at the same time.

Prep time: 15 minutes

Cooking time: 45 minutes

Servings: 6

2 beets, peeled and chopped into 1-inch cubes
4 large carrots, peeled and chopped into large pieces
1 turnip, peeled and chopped into large pieces

1 sweet potato, peeled and chopped into 1-inch cubes

1 large red onion, peeled and cut lengthwise into thick wedges

2 tablespoons olive oil

Fresh thyme, leaves removed from stem and quickly cut to release fragrant oils

Kosher salt

Fresh ground black pepper

Preheat the oven to 400°F if it's not already on.

Once you've peeled and chopped all the veggies, place them into a large bowl. Pour in about 2 tablespoons of olive oil, then add the fresh thyme and a couple of healthy pinches of kosher salt. Turn the pepper grinder about 5–6 times. Grab a spoon and mix around until everything is well coated. Add more salt, pepper, or thyme as needed.

Place a piece of parchment paper in a large sheet pan and dump out the veggies, spreading into an even layer. Move to the oven and bake for 45 minutes, but it may take up to an hour. Take them out and stir about halfway through.

Black Forest Cake

This recipe just feels like a great antidote to cold weather. Served with some tea, hot coffee, or another gin fizz, it will chase away the winter blues.

Prep time: 30 minutes

Cooking time: 45 minutes

Servings: 6 or 8, depending on how many slices you like

Cake

1 cup (2 sticks) unsalted butter, softened

2 cups granulated sugar

4 eggs, room temperature

3 cups cake flour

2 teaspoons baking powder

1½ teaspoons baking soda

¾ cup unsweetened cocoa powder

2 cups milk

2 teaspoons vanilla extract

Cherry Sauce

1 can (14 ounces) sour cherries, strain cherries and set aside, reserving the cherry juice for the sauce

½ cup granulated sugar

Whipped Cream

1 pint heavy whipping cream

½ cup confectioners' sugar

Preheat the oven to 350°F.

For the cake: In a stand mixer with the whisk attachment, put the butter and sugar in the bowl and mix until well incorporated. Add eggs one at a time, allowing them to fully incorporate before adding the next.

Meanwhile, in a medium bowl, add the cake flour, baking powder, baking soda, and cocoa powder, sifting together. Turn the mixer on low and slowly mix in the dry ingredients and milk. Finish off by adding the vanilla extract.

Prepare two 9-inch cake pans either by lining with a parchment circle or by rubbing butter onto the bottoms and sides of the pans and then sprinkling with flour and shaking it around until coated.

Pour in the cake batter, evenly dispersing between the two pans, and place them in the oven for 25–30 minutes, checking with a wooden toothpick for doneness. A toothpick inserted into the middle of your cake should come out clean.

Allow cakes to cool about 10 minutes before transferring to a wire rack to cool completely.

For the cherry sauce: Put the reserved cherry juice and extra ½ cup of sugar into a saucepan and put over medium heat until the sugar dissolves. Remove from heat and place 6–8 of the set-aside cherries in the sauce, which will be used for decorating.

For the whipped cream topping: In a stand mixer, attach the whisk attachment and pour the heavy whipping cream into the bowl. Start on the low setting and slowly increase to a medium speed to avoid splashing. When you see the cream start to firm up, stop and add the confectioners' sugar. Once again, start the whisk on a low setting and work up a little at a time in order to prevent the sugar from erupting from the bowl. Keep whisking until the cream has just set into soft peaks. If you overdo it, you'll have a very firm whipped cream that's less easy to spread.

Assembling the cake: Using a cake leveler or just a bread knife and a good eye, cut off the top of any dome that formed on your cakes while baking to help them stack more neatly. If your cakes had a nice rise in the oven, you may want to cut each in half horizontally, leaving you with four layers. This presentation can add to the wow factor of the cake, but you can also just stick to two layers, especially if you didn't get much of a rise.

Place the first layer on a serving platter or cake stand and gently brush with the cherry sauce and place a thin, even layer of whipped cream. Continue for each layer, making sure to reserve about half of the whipped cream to decorate the exterior of the cake. Use an angled cake spatula to evenly apply the whipped cream to the top and sides, aiming for an even, smooth application. Top with 6–8 cherries along the perimeter of the top of the cake, one for each slice that you'll be serving. Store in the refrigerator until ready to serve.

Gin Fizz

The gin fizz is a great way to start off the evening—a fun and bubbly introduction for your friends and family to set the mood.

Prep time: 3 minutes
Servings: 1

2 ounces of your favorite gin
1 ounce freshly squeezed lemon juice
1 ounce simple syrup
1 egg, white separated, yolk reserved for another recipe

1 can or bottle of club soda
Lemon peel, twisted if desired

In a cocktail shaker, add in the gin, lemon juice, simple syrup, and egg white. Shake vigorously without ice for at least 15 seconds to allow the egg white to be incorporated. Add a few ice cubes to the shaker and vigorously shake again, about 10 seconds. If you have a built-in strainer (called a *cobbler shaker*), pour through that and a cocktail strainer. If not, pour through your cocktail strainer and a fine mesh strainer. Serve in a Tom Collins glass (they're tall and narrow) and top off with club soda, reserving the unused soda for other guests. Garnish with a twist of lemon peel and enjoy! Happy Yule!

Crafty Crafts

Raechel Henderson

THE COMING OF YULE brings with it the promise of the end of darkness. After months of lengthening nights and lessening light, the tide has turned. With the end of the longest night of the year, the sun returns with the promise of the spring to come. But the days and nights leading up to Yule can be disheartening, especially to those who might suffer from seasonal affective disorder. To that end, extra light, especially in the form of candles, can help beat back the depressive energies of the season. The warm glow of candles softens the darkness and creates a cozy atmosphere.

Citrus Votive Holders

Create these citrus peel votive holders to bring solar energy into your space and combat the darkness of the days and weeks leading up to Yule.

Materials
Citrus fruits such as oranges, lemons, limes, etc.
Votive candles

Tools

A sharp knife
A citrus juicer
A small spoon
Towels
Cutting board
Optional: small vegetable shape cutters

Cost: $5–$15. The main cost will be in the citrus fruit. The vegetable shape cutters will range in price from $5 to $10 depending on where you get them from and how many you buy.

Time spent: 1 hour. This includes the actual making of the votive holder and allowing it to dry a little before use.

While all citrus fruits are associated with solar energy, each particular fruit has its own magical properties that are distinct from the others:

- Grapefruits are associated with purification and mental clarity.
- Lemons are associated with purification, love, and friendship.
- Limes are associated with healing, love, and protection.
- Oranges are associated with love, luck, and abundance.
- Tangerines are associated with healing, love, and protection.

Choose a citrus fruit aligned with your magical goals. If you could use a better-paying job, pick up an orange. Need to be able to think clearly? Choose a grapefruit. When looking at what fruit to use, choose one that is ripe and without imperfections in the peel. Also go for fruits that aren't oddly shaped.

While you are working on this craft, think about what your magical goals are. Visualize your citrus votive holder enhancing and supporting your actions to bring those goals to fruition. For example, if you are looking to bring love into your life, imagine placing the votive next to you when you're browsing dating apps. Envision the loving vibrations from the lemon peel guiding your matches.

You can use vegetable cutters to punch out shapes in your votive holder, or freehand the cutouts with a sharp knife. Cut heart shapes for love, circles for solar energy, stars for wishes, etc. You can also carve words to represent your magical intentions, such as "love," "protection," "money," and so on. Save the cutouts to make the citrus peel garland below to amplify the solar energy in your home.

Instructions

Start by creating sacred space to work in according to your path. Cut the citrus fruit widthwise so that you have a top and bottom half. Using the juicer, remove the inside fruit from the peel. You can save the juice to use as a marinade for meat or add it to cocktails to bring that solar energy into your body.

Next, use the spoon to scrape out the membrane and any pulp that was left behind. Be careful not to poke a hole into the peel. Tip: scrape from the bottom to the top edge of the peel for best results.

Wash the peel with cold water and then dry it inside and out with a towel. At this point, you may need to slice off the bottom layer of your citrus fruit so that it sits flat. Make sure not to cut through the white pith of the peel.

Use the vegetable-shape cutters or the knife to make cutouts around the sides of the citrus peel. Cut from the inside out. Set the peel on a towel and let dry for an hour or more. Afterward, place votive candles inside the holder and set them on your altar or use as decoration throughout your home.

Citrus Peel Garland

There is no need to throw away the citrus peel cutouts. Instead, follow the directions below to make a sweet solar energy garland that you can wrap on your tree or hang over your altar.

Materials
Peel cutouts from the Citrus Votive Holders craft above
Twine

Tools
A wooden skewer
Large-eyed needle, like a tapestry needle

Cost: $5–$10. The main cost will be from the twine, skewer, and needle if you don't already have them on hand.

Time spent: 30 minutes

Instructions
Start by creating sacred space to work in according to your path. Gather up the citrus peel cutouts and, using the wooden skewer, poke a hole at the top of each one.

Thread the twine through a large-eyed needle and run the twine through the hole in the cutouts. As you do so, think upon what it

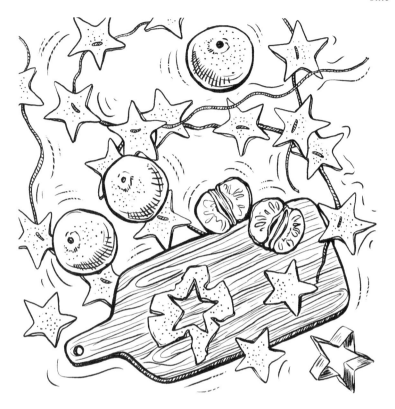

is that you want to bring into your life this Yule and beyond. Are you looking to change careers? Find love? Maybe you just want to work on your inner peace and contentment. Whatever your goals, envision each little cutout as your own personal cheerleader. Citrus fruits are filled with active, manifesting energy. They will help propel your intentions forward to completion.

Ensure that there are at least twelve inches of twine before the first cutout and after the last. Arrange the cutouts along the twine so that they are at equal distances apart. Once you have threaded all the cutouts on the twine, tie a loop on either end of the twine so that you can hang the garland. When you tie your knots, release the energy that you've been working with to the universe.

Hang your garland on your tree or over your altar. The peels will dry as they hang. Every time you look upon it, know that your magical goals will work out because you have solar, citrus energy fueling them. Once Yule is over and you start changing out your altar, discard the garland by either burying or burning it. You can make another when the Wheel of the Year once again turns toward Yule.

Yule Meditations

Elizabeth Barrette

AT THE DARKEST TIME of the year, Yule sprinkles the world with colorful lights and holiday cheer. It reminds us that no matter how dark and cold things get, they don't stay that way forever, and there are always bright spots to find. Meditations for Yule should be suitable for indoor work. This is a great time for the colorful practice of chakra meditation. However, if you feel overloaded by all the noisy, blinking attractions, then you can try focusing on just one thing at a time.

Chakra Meditation

Chakras are energy nodes. Think of them kind of like joints in your energy—or your personal string of holiday lights! The seven main chakras align with your central nervous system in a column from the base of your spine going up to your head, following the rainbow from red up to violet. There are also minor chakras elsewhere, such as your major joints and the palms of your hands.

These nodes maintain the flow of energy through your body. If something goes wrong with them, it can manifest as physical or emotional problems. Conversely, illnesses or injuries to part of your self can impact the chakras. Ideally, they should all be open moderately and at about the same level. If a chakra is overactive, underactive, or blocked, then it can not only mess up that part of your self but may also distort other chakras. So it's important to keep them working properly.

This makes chakra meditation more complicated than most other types. First, you have to examine your chakras to see what they are doing. Then, if there are problems, you have to work on those. Some people like a rainbow chakra wall hanging, wand, or pendant to help follow the steps.

The root chakra relates to physicality. Blockages may come from stress, health worries, or money issues and may manifest as pelvic discomfort, difficulty concentrating, or poor grounding.

The sacral chakra governs sexuality and pleasure. Blockages can stem from sexual mistreatment or resistance to joy and typically manifest as difficulty connecting with new people or malfunctions of the reproductive or eliminatory organs.

The solar plexus chakra centers on the stomach. Blockages could come from gaslighting or not being able to "stomach" disturbing things and often manifest as a lack of confidence, digestive upsets, or skin problems.

The heart chakra governs the heart and lungs. Blockages may come from toxic relationships or chest injuries and tend to manifest as difficulty feeling and expressing love, immune system failures, or circulatory issues.

The throat chakra rules communication. Blockages can come from self-censorship, secrets, or oppression and commonly manifest as difficulty speaking or expressing thoughts and illnesses of the throat or mouth.

The third eye chakra concerns the psyche. Blockages could stem from distraction, anxiety, or head injury and often manifest as lack of purpose, headaches, or eye issues.

The crown chakra connects to your higher self. Blockages can come from burnout or disconnection between body and spirit, typically manifesting as stress, exhaustion, and sleep disturbances.

For chakra meditation, lie flat on your back. Breathe slowly and deeply. Focus on your body and its energy nodes. Beginning at your feet, observe the flow moving through your center line. Check each chakra in turn for proper function. If overactive, close it down a bit; if underactive, open it up more. If blocked, seek the cause so you can work it loose. Healing blockages takes time and effort, usually requiring multiple sessions. Regular chakra meditation maintains proper flow and minimizes the risk of malfunctions.

Concentrative Meditation

Concentrative meditation is also known as *object meditation*. It is the skill of staying focused on one thing to the exclusion of all else, narrowing your attention to a single point. Essentially, you fill up your whole mind with that object so there is no room for anything else. This is a very useful skill to develop, as you can also use it for practical tasks outside of meditation.

This practice is simple but difficult to maintain. Many obstacles get in the way. Pleasure and desire draw the mind toward nicer thoughts. Physical restlessness and mental worries undermine the sense of calm. Sluggishness and procrastination interfere with actually sitting down to meditate. Doubt of the self, the practice, or other things can disrupt focus, which requires determination.

In order to cultivate concentration, you must be patient. Don't strain yourself trying to force it. That's like pushing on a rope. This is not a competition. It is an exercise, strengthening your concentration like you would strengthen a muscle. Just keep working at it, and you will make progress. Pay attention to obstacles; once you identify yours, then you can work on overcoming them.

This is a case where "just do it" is sound advice: apply your butt to your meditation cushion and keep it there. In the beginning, short sessions work better to create a sense of success. You may only be able to hold your focus for a minute or so. A good minute is better than a bad ten minutes. You may wish to attempt this several times a day to get in more practice.

On the bright side, concentrative meditation is portable. You can pick any object, including one that will fit in your pocket or can be worn. If you're stuck waiting, whip it out and meditate for a minute. You could also select a random object in view whenever you need one. Ideally, choose something memorable with distinctive features so that it's easy to keep your eyes on it.

For concentrative meditation, it's best to sit upright and cross-legged on the floor or straight in a chair. The little bit of physical effort required to maintain this position will help you stay alert. Lying down, you might fall asleep. Take a few deep breaths. Slow down and seek a state of calm. This will make it easier to narrow your focus. Bring your attention to your focal object. Concentrate on it so that everything else fades away. Ignore other thoughts or feelings for now. In this moment, you only care about the object. Whenever your mind tries to drift, firmly bring it back to your focus.

Avoid examination, analysis, or interpretation. The point is not to think *about* the object, just to regard it as it is. Do not follow or engage with any other ideas. Exist without judgment or distraction. There is only your concentration and the object it rests upon. This is difficult. You can learn to do it anyway.

During the busy holiday season, take time for yourself. Meditation can help you relax and recharge.

Yule Ritual

Irene Glasse

THIS YULE RITUAL INVITES blessings to the home with sigils, candlelight, and sound. Sunwait candles can be used, or create a new set of candles for the ritual. As the longest night passes, we release what does not serve and invite new energy into our lives. The increasing light of each lit candle reminds us of the promise of Yule and the brighter days ahead.

Sunlight, Sigils, and Sound

In this Yule ritual, we will use candles, sigils, and sound to bless our home. This ritual should be performed at sunset on Yule.

You will need

Six traditional flame candles or battery-powered flicker candles large enough to draw, paint, or inscribe with one of the six sigils. If you have been practicing Sunwait, you may use your Sunwait candles.

Six sigils, each representing a different blessing you'd like to bring into your life in the coming year. You can use existing sigils like runes or ogham or create your own.

An altar holding a lighter and snuffer if you are using flame candles,
a bell or rattle, and any additional altar decorations you would
like to include. Altar decorations are lovely but optional and entirely up to you.

A snack and drink. For Yule, I like to use fresh bread, smoked or
cured meats, aged cheeses, dried fruit like dates, and mulled
cider.

Optional: candleholders if you are using traditional flame candles,
journaling supplies.

Prepare for the ritual by selecting or creating the six sigils or
symbols you would like to use. Paint, draw, or inscribe one sigil on
each candle. As you do so, focus on the meaning of the sigil. If the
sigil has a name, you can chant or sing it while you are applying it
to the candle.

Bathe and dress for the ritual in the manner you prefer. I like
to wear green and gold for Yule, and I include a sun pendant in my
jewelry. If you have purification practices (anointing, saining with
smoke, asperging with water, etc.), perform those as well.

Set up your altar with the six unlit candles, candleholders,
lighter, snuffer, bell or rattle, any other decorations or supplies you
would like to have on hand, and food and drink. If it is possible,
crack a window open near your altar just enough to allow energy to
depart.

Welcome any guides, guardians, deities, and benevolent ancestors you'd like to include in your ritual.

Ring the bell or shake the rattle and say:

The sun sets on the shortest day;
The longest night is here.
[I/we] welcome Yule into [my/our] home
And honor a new solar year.
The night is long and dark tonight
But warm and safe within.

[I/we] welcome blessings to [my/our] home
And to all who dwell herein.

Walk through the rooms you wish to cleanse with the rattle or bell, shaking or ringing it. Visualize the sound breaking up and releasing any stuck energy from the darkest days of winter. If moving around is challenging, simply visualize the sound of the rattle or bell reaching all areas you wish to purify. If you would like, you can say something like this to guide the energy you are releasing to depart:

The light is coming, shadows flee.
Take your path away from me.
The year is turning, go in peace.
With this sound you are released.

When you have finished, return to your altar and close the window if you have opened one.

Pick up the first candle and contemplate the sigil on it and what it means to you. If you are performing this ritual with others, invite them to share their thoughts on the sigil as well. If the sigil has a name, begin to sing or chant it. If it does not have a name, choose one of the qualities your sigil represents (abundance, peace, health, etc.) and begin to sing or chant that word.

Light the candle (or turn it on if it's battery-powered) and carefully carry the candle through all the rooms you wish its blessing to touch, chanting the sigil's name or qualities as you walk. Imagine the sound of your voice and the light of the candle filling your home with the blessing of the sigil. If moving around is challenging, simply visualize the light of the candle and sound of your voice reaching all areas you wish to bless.

Carefully carry the lit candle back to your altar and set it down. Pick up the second candle and begin the pattern again: contemplate the sigil and discuss its meaning with any ritual participants. Begin to sing or chant the sigil's name or quality and light the candle. Carefully carry the lit candle through the rooms you are blessing while singing or chanting. When you have finished, bring the lit candle back to the altar and set it down.

Repeat this process with the remaining four candles. When you have returned the final candle to the altar, sit down and contemplate the light of the six lit candles. Feel their glow spreading energetically throughout your home.

Enjoy the food and drink you set out for yourself. Eat mindfully—feasting is traditional at Yuletide and a way to connect with the centuries of Yule celebrations stretching back through history.

When you have finished eating, contemplate the feeling of the blessings around you and the shining light of the candles against the dark night outside. When you are ready to end the ritual, say:

With sound and sigil, [I/we] welcome light.
The returning sun [I/we] honor;
Every day shall grow more bright
Like these candles on the altar.
As the year toward summer turns,
Hope stirs within [my/our] heart(s),
And blessings of the sun's return
[I/We] weave into [my/our] hearth

Ring the bell or shake the rattle. Offer gratitude to any guides, guardians, deities, or benevolent ancestors you invited to join you for the ritual. You may allow the candles to continue burning for a time or snuff them. You may remain in contemplation for a while, write down any reflections, or simply begin to clean up your ritual supplies and return your living space to its usual layout.

May the returning sun bless you with joy, hope, and abundance. Blessed Yule!

Notes

Notes

Imbolc

The Creative Threshold

Sara Mellas

LIKE ALL CROSS-QUARTER DAYS, Imbolc is a marker of the in-between. It's a time of liminality, defined as a state of existing between one place and another. This often feels uncomfortable in the context of modern existence; it is far easier to cling to the clarity and perceived certainty that come with absolutes. Whether literal, like the midpoint between the winter solstice and spring equinox, or figurative, like the time that stretches between one phase of life and the next, liminality can feel unstable, disorienting, and unpredictable. And yet, the root of the word, *limin*, means "threshold."

Imbolc is so much more than a departure from winter and a preparation for spring; it is a holiday that asks us to honor how we've arrived at a threshold and to welcome the new beginnings that await us.

Darkness and Light

The polarity of darkness and light is an integral part of existence, as nature demonstrates to us each and every day. During the days of Imbolc, February 1 and 2, the darkness of winter still feels very much present throughout most of the Northern Hemisphere. And yet, it's on these days we celebrate the return of the light. We know its arrival will be gradual and put our trust in the promise of longer, lighter days. Despite the dark, our awareness of being at this threshold of light instills us with hope and readiness.

Just as nature's vitality depends on cycles of darkness and light, our lives unfold to these rhythms as well. A balance of the two is so necessary to our energy and creativity, and yet we can be quick to assign value judgments of negative and positive, instinctually resisting the dark and clinging to the light.

The time between Yule and Imbolc is one of stillness, reflection, and restoration; it's imperative to new growth. It's a reminder that when we experience darker times in our personal lives, there is a clearing occurring within us, no matter how subtle or imperceptible it may be in the present. By cultivating an awareness of this and releasing resistance, we remember that in time we will enter a figurative Imbolc. Our experience will shift into a liminal space that may still feel quite dark but in truth is the threshold of a new beginning with renewed vitality, creativity, and light.

In this space, we are given an opportunity to lean into the journey of transition, to allow anticipation and trust to take the place of fear and uncertainty. The light will return, and in the liminality of Imbolc, we're empowered to decide how we want to greet it.

Astrology and Imbolc

Each year, Imbolc occurs while the Sun is moving through the sign of Aquarius, meaning that the corresponding New and Full Moons occur in Aquarius and Leo, respectively. For as above, so below; it is no coincidence that the intention and energy of Imbolc is an expression of its place in the astrological cycle.

One of the most central tenets of the Leo-Aquarius axis is creativity. Leo relates to self-expression, personal creativity, and performance, while Aquarius governs creative collaboration, creative thinking, and innovation. Leo focuses on the individual, while Aquarius emphasizes the collective. In this way, Leo considers how creative contributions impact the collective, while from an opposing perspective, Aquarius assesses how collective creative efforts effect the individual.

Leo, ruled by the Sun, is the brightest fire of the zodiac, and Aquarius, ruled by Saturn (traditional) and Uranus (modern), is a chill burst of air. Astrologically, the pairing of fire and air is visionary energy, and both Leo and Aquarius relate to visions of the future—Aquarius quite literally, as it possesses the innovative, eccentric, and forward-thinking rationality to envision and plan for a better future. Leo on the other hand generates things in the present that live on past the lives of the people who made them, whether in the form of creative works or children.

This year's Imbolc is exceptionally powerful, as it occurs on the day after the Full Moon, taking place at 13 degrees of Leo on February 1, 2026, at 5:09 p.m. EST. Believe it or not, the last time a Full Moon happened during Imbolc was in 1551! Experiencing the fullest light of the Moon on this celebration is not to be taken for granted; this is an incredibly supportive energy with which to invite in Imbolc blessings.

While there are many things to be said about the astrological signature of this Full Moon, perhaps the most significant is that while the Sun and Moon are opposite one another, Neptune will be situated at 0 degrees of Aries. Neptune is the planet that rules over creativity, dreams, visions, illusions, liminal spaces, other realms, psychic ability, visual arts, and the sea. Zero degrees Aries is the very beginning of the astrological cycle, the start of the 360-degree wheel of the zodiac. As such, when planets transit this degree, they begin a new journey.

The speed of a planet's orbit determines how quickly it takes this journey before returning to 0 degrees Aries to start anew. For instance, the Moon does so roughly every 29 days and the Sun every 365 days. Neptune, however, is a slow-moving planet and takes about 165 *years* to complete a full cycle.

On February 1, not only will Neptune be supercharged with the initiating energy of beginning a brand new zodiacal cycle, this will be the first Full Moon in Leo occurring with Neptune in Aries since 1863. There is abundant potential for seeding new creative ideas on this Imbolc and for using our intuition to devise strategies for bringing our creativity to light.

Creativity and Intuition

Traditionally, Imbolc has been a celebration to honor the goddess Brigid, who in Celtic mythology is associated with healing, fertility, poetry, blacksmithing, divination, and prophecy. Like most mythological goddesses, she is a channel of creativity and regeneration, represented by the fire and sacred flame with which she is so often depicted.

Many of us have been socialized to think of creativity as a quality that exists inside of us, one that some individuals possess more than others, and that is typically expressed through artistic pursuits. I find this notion to be an extremely limiting and restrictive assessment of what creativity is and what it means to live creatively.

All we need to do is look at the natural world that surrounds us to see proof that creativity is a force of its own, possessed by no one. There is an abundance of generative energy that wants to move through each and every one of us, and the more we work with it, the more light we bring into our collective existence. Creativity is universal; it's how we use it that is individual. To be creative is to momentarily work with this universal energy in a way that is personal, then to release it back into the universe in a renewed form for all to experience and share.

I believe creativity flows in a constant state of desire to be invited in, that it seeks out the individuals who are eager and open to working with it. All one needs to be creative is a spirit of curiosity and a willingness to listen. When we show up intrigued and receptive, creativity speaks to us through our intuition.

Intuition and creativity are inextricably linked, as they both exist in liminal space. Intuition is a bridge between source and our lived experience in the physical realm. It connects us to the past, present, and future, helping us uncover our individual truths in the context of shared time and space. This space between source and the physical realm is also where creativity abides, and it's always waiting to meet us on the bridge of intuition.

How we manifest creativity into the physical realm is unique to each individual. For some, it may be artistic, musical, a performance, or a piece of writing. It may be starting a business, an organization, or creating community. It may be so profound as birthing a child. To others, personal creativity may be more abstract, like adopting a new way of thinking or approaching one's life and endeavors in a nontraditional or previously unexplored way. This cross quarter is an invitation to trust your intuition when it reveals how creativity wants to be expressed through you.

Inward to the Light

While outward offerings, ritual, and celebration are an integral part of the cross-quarter holidays, Imbolc reminds us to also go inward. It reassures us of the meaning and necessity of liminal space, inviting us to connect with our intuition and discover the spark of creativity that's within, awaiting our attention. This is the time to step out of the dark and brave the liminality in which creativity has come to find us. In this space, we can begin stoking the creative flames and living by the light of our own sacred fire.

Cosmic Sway

Michael Herkes

As the Wheel of the Year turns, we find ourselves in that magical time between winter and spring. From February 2 to March 20, 2026, the stars and planets dance in ways that offer us unique opportunities for growth and reflection.

Observing Imbolc

Imbolc kicks things off on February 2, right after the Full Moon shines in Leo. It's like the universe is giving us a double dose of fiery energy to shake off the winter blues. Imbolc has always been about welcoming back the light, and with Leo in the mix, it's a perfect time to let your own inner light shine too. To celebrate this combining energy, light a white, yellow, orange, or gold candle, brew some warm milk and honey, and savor them as you meditate about what you want to grow in your life as the days get longer.

New Moon in Aquarius and Lunar New Year

Just a couple of weeks later, we've got the New Moon in Aquarius on February 17 at 7:01 a.m., lining up perfectly with the Lunar New Year, kicking off the Year of the Horse. It's like the universe is giving us a cosmic high five and saying, "Hey, time for a fresh start!"

Now, Aquarius energy is all about shaking things up and thinking outside the box. It's that friend who always has the wildest ideas but somehow makes them work. This New Moon is perfect for dreaming big and maybe even starting that project you've been putting off. You know, the one that could make a real difference in your community?

And then we've got the Year of the Horse galloping in. In Chinese astrology, the Horse is like that free spirit who's always up for an adventure. It's bringing a vibe of "Let's do this!" to the whole year ahead.

If you're looking for spellwork, this is a great time to focus on breaking free from whatever's been holding you back. Maybe light a candle and write down some goals, or create a little ritual to boost your confidence. Horse energy is perfect for spells about travel, getting physically stronger, or just pushing yourself to try new things.

The cool thing about this combo is how the thoughtful, innovative side of Aquarius mixes with the bold, adventurous spirit of the Horse. It's like having your head in the clouds but your feet ready to run. You could use this energy to plan something big—maybe a trip you've always wanted to take or a new project that scares you a little (in a good way).

Whatever you decide to do, remember that this is a powerful time for new beginnings. So dream big, be bold, and get ready for a year of exciting changes!

Surviving Mercury Retrograde in Pisces

But hold on to your hats, because Mercury's about to go retrograde in Pisces from February 26 to March 20. I know, I know, Mercury retrograde gets a bad rap. But it's not all doom and gloom. Sure, you might want to double-check your emails and be extra clear when talking to folks, but it's also a great time to slow down and reflect. Pisces energy is dreamy and intuitive, so why not use this time to dive deep into your feelings or maybe try some meditation?

During this retrograde, it's essential to work on balancing the emotional depth of Pisces with the need for clear communication. Avoid making major decisions or signing contracts, and instead, use this time for introspection and healing. Pisces is a sign connected to the spiritual realm, so this is an excellent time for meditation, dream work, and reconnecting with your intuition.

Here are some tips for surviving Mercury retrograde in Pisces:

- Ground yourself daily: Practice grounding techniques such as walking barefoot on the earth, carrying grounding stones like hematite or black tourmaline, or meditating to connect with your root chakra.
- Be mindful in communication: Double-check your messages, emails, and agreements. Clarify any misunderstandings and avoid jumping to conclusions.
- Use water as a healing tool: As Pisces is a water sign, incorporate water into your spiritual practice. Take cleansing baths, use water scrying, or work with the element of water in rituals to wash away confusion and emotional clutter.
- Work with Pisces energy: Embrace the intuitive, creative, and spiritual aspects of Pisces. This retrograde is a powerful time for deep healing, letting go of old emotional wounds, and connecting with the Divine.

March Moon Magic

As we move into March, we've got two more Moons to work with. There's a Full Moon in Virgo on March 3 at 6:38 a.m., which is perfect for getting organized and focused in the center of Mercury retrograde. The Full Moon in Virgo brings practical, grounded energy to help us manifest our intentions in a tangible way. Virgo, an earth sign, is all about structure, routine, and attention to detail. After the dreamy retrograde in Pisces, this Virgo Full Moon is a breath of fresh air, helping us regain focus and clarity.

Use this Full Moon to cleanse and organize your space, body, and mind. Engage in rituals that promote health, well-being, and efficiency. Virgo is also ruled by Mercury, so this Full Moon can help bring clarity to any confusion or miscommunication caused by the retrograde. It's a great time for detoxifying both physically and spiritually, cutting out what no longer serves you.

Then, on March 18 at 9:23 p.m., we round things out with a New Moon back in Pisces. It's like the universe is giving us one more chance to tap into our intuition before spring really kicks in.

Summary

As we wrap up this magical journey from Imbolc to the cusp of spring, we're reminded of the ever-changing dance of energies that shape our world. This period from February to March offers a unique blend of fiery inspiration, innovative thinking, and deep introspection.

From the warmth of Imbolc's candles to the dreamy waters of Pisces, we've explored ways to harness these cosmic energies for personal growth and spiritual practice. Whether it's setting bold intentions with the Aquarius New Moon, grounding ourselves during Mercury retrograde, or finding clarity with the Virgo Full Moon, each celestial event offers its own lessons and opportunities.

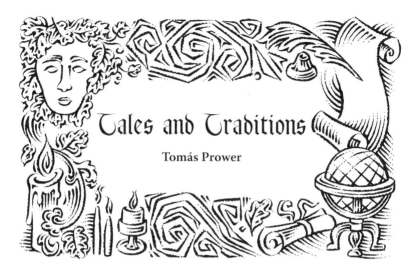

Tales and Traditions

Tomás Prower

Imbolc marks the beginning of spring and, really, beginnings in general. It is a time to start thinking about the planting season soon ahead and the new generations of lambs and calves about to be born. Just as much, it is a time for us to do some spring cleaning to clear out the old, dusty clutter that we accumulated over the winter and get exercising again from the stagnation of the cold months. That way we can enjoy spring and summer with vim, vigor, and gusto. This is the time when our New Year's resolutions are really put to the test. With January done and gone, are we still keeping our promises to ourselves? And if we are not, then how much of a fresh start do we really want for ourselves? How much do we really want our lives to be different from last year? Are they just desires and would-be-nice hopes? Or are we meeting the Universe halfway and showing active faith in their fulfillment by dedicating action toward the new lives we want?

Maman Brigitte: A Fresh Taste of Medicine

Traditionally, in Wicca and other magic-focused religions and world outlooks inspired by the traditional folklore of Western Europe, Imbolc is associated with the Celtic deity Brigid, a goddess who holds patronage over, among other things, healing. Through the eras, Christian missionaries came to the Celtic lands and converted the local peoples, syncretizing their old deities with Catholic saints. Thus, Brigid became Saint Brigid, who also held patronage over many of the same dominions, including healing. But now she also came with a new backstory of being the abbess of a nunnery in Ireland. Of course, Brigid's syncretized transformations didn't end there, for over in the New World, enslaved peoples were rebelliously and subversively reverse-syncretizing her again as an aesthetic mask covering their traditional deities, whom they could not revere or worship in public.

Enter Maman Brigitte (*Maman* being French for "Mama" or "Mom"), the syncretization of a traditional African deity with Saint Brigid among the enslaved peoples in the French colonies of the Americas. Again, like Brigid and Saint Brigid, Maman Brigitte also holds patronage over healing, though her medicine is always a bit more intense. Nevertheless, her medicine is just as potent and effective as her penchant for spices and flavors of acquired taste. Moreover, the healing of Maman Brigitte extends over into the spiritual realm, healing our minds and spirits in addition to our bodies.

This spiritual healing comes from her dominion as a psychopomp deity, guiding the souls of the deceased to the lands that lay beyond. And if Imbolc is the time of year for Brigid and her healing grace, it is even more so the time of year for Maman Brigitte and her more robust medicine of body and mind. After all, it takes quite the energy and willpower to start a new life, because the results in our life are the summation of all our daily habits. Unlike medicine to heal the body, healing a bad habit involves mental medicine. Replacing a bad habit with a good habit requires a strong and sustained mental shift in our habitual way of thinking, in our lack of self-discipline, and in our modes of autopilot that seek out the easiest and most comforting choices in life rather than the more difficult yet healthier ones.

You want to be healthier? Well, diet and exercise are fantastic, but the key to diet and exercise is consistency. It's not how healthily you eat or how hard you work out in a single day; it's how consistently you eat healthily and work out. You want to develop a new skill like painting, playing an instrument, or coding computers? Again, how consistently you practice, not how intensely you dive into it for only a day or two, will determine how far you will develop that skill. And this is one of the spiritual lessons of Imbolc: How dedicated are you to the new life you want? How attached are you to the old life you've had?

The medicine of Maman Brigitte is especially apt for this endeavor into the new calendar year. Unlike her saintly counterpart from Ireland, demure and soft, Maman Brigitte is an outspoken badass. She'll puff on a cigar while speaking truth to power and sip on spiced rum as she reads your self-imposed pretense to filth. This more assertive and hard-edged aspect to Maman Brigitte coincidentally (or perhaps not so coincidentally, as mythology tends to prove) emerged from the way in which the enslaved peoples of the New World chose Saint Brigid as the aesthetic mask for Maman Brigitte.

In New Orleans in particular, enslaved women from Africa were often forced to work backbreaking large construction projects, such as building levees. Alongside them, and, at times, replacing them in these difficult and arduous tasks, were female indentured servants from Ireland. These Irish women were no high-class ladies, and their hard lives at the bottom of the social ladder made them no strangers to foul language, bawdy jokes, or open vice. Thus, not only Maman Brigitte's name but also her hard-drinking, hard-living indulgence of base pleasures and disregard for pretentious social mores, as well as her redheaded white complexion, owed much to these Irish servants who labored alongside enslaved African women in those Southern swamps, an apropos syncretized mask behind which Vodouisants could continue their traditions.

It's Maman Brigitte's straight-shooting nature that will truly change your life. She'll tell you how it is without sugarcoating it to make it more palatable. After all, how can you change a bad habit if you don't acknowledge it directly? Your mental medicine involves being fully honest with yourself about all the limiting beliefs, excuses, and bull that you stagnate yourself with to prevent true, lasting change.

Beware, because stagnation is comfortably seductive. Yes, you may not like where you are in life right now, but at least it's familiar as opposed to all the frightening unknowns that come with a new life. But stagnation is death both of the body and of the soul. The stiff, hard-to-move rigor mortis is a calling card of death, and Maman Brigitte knows this all too intimately. So if you want to live, move. Bend and twist and turn and change. And why not start now? Although yesterday was the best day to begin, today, Imbolc, is the next best day to make a magical commitment to yourself to take that medicine, swallow it down, and establish a fresh start to your new life by building new habits. After all, the time will pass whether or not you do anything, so why not do something?

Feasts and Treats

Nathan M. Hall

While I'm in some of the warmest parts of Florida, I still manage to make a chili once or twice a year when the weather cools as much as it's going to here. Imbolc for me is about keeping that flame lit that started at Yule, honoring Brighid, and having a nice, comforting meal. The brownies are a bit indulgent, but hey, it's still winter, right? You need those calories to keep you warm!

Chili

This recipe can be made a day ahead to both enhance the flavors of the chili and to give you the requisite time for the No-Knead Bread recipe, which pairs very well with it. Substitute an extra can of beans to make this vegetarian.

Prep time: 30 minutes

Cooking time: 65 minutes, but the longer you simmer, the richer the flavor will be

Servings: 6–8

Olive oil

1 pound ground beef or turkey

1 red onion, peeled and diced

1 tablespoon kosher salt, more to taste

3 garlic cloves, minced
1 28-ounce can stewed tomatoes
1 14-ounce can beef broth (substitute chicken or vegetable if desired)
1 1-ounce square baker's chocolate, roughly chopped
¼ cup tomato paste
1 tablespoon Worcestershire sauce
1 tablespoon ground cumin
2 teaspoons ground coriander
2 teaspoons onion powder
2 teaspoons ground paprika
2 teaspoons ground black pepper
1 teaspoon garlic powder
1 teaspoon red pepper flakes
½ teaspoon cayenne powder
1 14-ounce can black beans
1 14-ounce can kidney beans
Sour cream
Shredded sharp cheddar cheese
Chopped cilantro

Put a 6-quart pot or Dutch oven over medium-high heat, adding a splash of olive oil as well as the beef or turkey, or skip the meat and add another can of beans. Break up the meat while it's cooking so you end up with a medium crumble. Once the meat is browned but still not completely cooked through, push it to one side and drop in the diced red onion and a pinch of kosher salt, cooking in the excess oil and stirring regularly until it starts to become translucent. Add in the garlic and let cook until fragrant.

Put the can of stewed tomatoes in and stir, breaking up the tomatoes into smaller pieces. Pour in the can of broth and add the baker's chocolate and tomato paste. Add the rest of the kosher salt, Worcestershire sauce, and all of the spices. Stir and bring up to a boil before reducing to a simmer. Cover and let cook for about 30 minutes.

Add in the black beans and kidney beans and cook for 15 more minutes. If you're making a day ahead, allow to cool and put it in the refrigerator until you're ready to eat.

Garnish with sour cream, cheddar cheese, and cilantro, or whatever your favorite additions are.

No-Knead Bread

The smell of bread baking in the oven is the aroma of home. It creates its own magick, and much like a sweeten-up spell, it can calm rifts in the household and bring everyone together.

Prep time: 15 minutes

Proofing time: 12–24 hours (If you're in a hotter climate, favor a shorter proof.)

Cooking time: 40–45 minutes

Servings: 10–12

1 teaspoon active dry yeast
Pinch of light brown sugar
1½ cups, plus 1 tablespoon warm water
3 cups all-purpose flour (King Arthur is my favorite.)
1 teaspoon sea salt

In a large bowl, stir the yeast, brown sugar, and 1 tablespoon warm water together and let sit for about 10 minutes. Mix in the rest of the ingredients, including the remaining 1½ cups of warm water, with a spatula until combined and cover with plastic wrap. It will not look like a neat and uniform ball of dough but something monstrous and potentially threatening. Let it sit and come to life for the next day or so.

When your dough friend has sat for a sufficient amount of time, roll out some parchment paper and dust it with a generous amount of flour. With wet hands, remove the dough from the bowl and begin forming it into a ball, folding the sides under. If it starts sticking to you too much, just wet your hands again. Move the dough, parchment and all, back to the (cleaned) bowl and cover with a towel to rest for another couple hours.

About an hour and a half later, place a Dutch oven or an oven-safe pot and lid into the oven, set for 450°F. Once it's reached temperature, open the oven and take the lid off of your pot. Remove the parchment and dough from the bowl, using the parchment to lift and then gently deposit both into the pot. Return the lid to the pot and bake for 30 minutes. Remove the lid and bake for 10–15 more minutes until the top is a deep, golden brown.

Remove from the oven and from the pot and allow to cool on a wire rack on the counter. Cut generous slices for your guests and serve with a nice Irish-style butter alongside the chili.

Fudge Brownies

Irresistible, slightly chewy, and a heap of calories to help keep you warm for the remainder of the winter. I won't tell if you have more than one.

Prep time: 10 minutes
Cooking time: 25–40 minutes
Servings: 9

3 eggs
2 teaspoons vanilla extract
2 cups sugar
12-ounce package semi-sweet chocolate chips
1½ cups salted butter, plus more for baking dish
1½ cups flour
Optional: 1 teaspoon cinnamon to liven things up

Preheat oven to 325°F and grease a 10 × 10-inch glass baking dish with butter.

In a stand mixer, whisk together the eggs, vanilla, and sugar until just incorporated. Place the chocolate chips and butter into a microwave-safe dish and microwave for 20–30 seconds, removing and stirring to inspire melting and combining. Allow to cool just enough so that when you add it to the egg mixture it doesn't start cooking the egg. Combine the chocolate and butter mix with the egg and sugar mix; don't overwork it. Add the cinnamon, if using, to the flour and mix well, then add to the wet mix of ingredients, again slowly stirring until just combined.

Bake for up to 40 minutes, but begin checking at 25 minutes for doneness. You want it to be moist in the center but not raw. Remove from the oven and let it cool before covering and letting it sit overnight. Store in an airtight container at room temperature. Good luck keeping them around for more than a day or two!

Crafty Crafts

Raechel Henderson

IMBOLC SEES THE FIRST stirrings of spring. Translated as "ewe's milk," this is the time when lambs are born, early flowers such as snowdrops and crocuses bloom, and ice and snow melt under the heat of days that grow longer. Brigid, the Irish goddess turned Catholic saint, is associated with this sabbat. Her focus on fertility and life speaks to the promise of hope that Imbolc brings.

Spiral Incense Holder

The spiral is one of the most enduring images associated with Imbolc. The Wheel of the Year continues to spin, revealing the seasons in their time. And Imbolc sees the continuation of this spiral as winter's hold begins to break, heralding the return of spring.

This craft uses the spiral's form to create an incense holder for your altar. You can use it to tap into that constantly renewing energy of Imbolc. The fact that the clay is moldable, and that you can reshape it if you don't like how it turns out the first time, makes it perfect for Imbolc, which is a time of new beginnings. Nothing is yet set in stone, and you can continue to shape and mold the clay until you are happy with the way it turned out.

You can decorate the spiral with crystals, stones, shells, and more to enhance the energies of Imbolc. Some suggestions for crystals include amethyst for protection, moonstone for transition, and carnelian for vitality.

Just like magic, crafting is the act of bringing your intentions into reality. As such, take some time to think about how you want to decorate your incense holder before you get started. Imbolc's energies range from fertility to rebirth to the end of winter, all of which you can tap into. Consider a theme for your incense holder. Maybe you want to keep with your New Year's resolutions (rebirth), and so for that you might include red jasper or clear quartz crystals. Maybe you want to bring more abundance into your life, so you add a coin to represent that.

As you are working the clay and shaping it into the spiral, think about what Imbolc means to you. What does renewal look like in your life? Is there something you'd like to start over? What new projects or outlooks would you like to begin now that it's the end of winter and the start of spring?

Materials
White air-dry clay
Crystals
Shells
Stones
Optional: gesso, acrylic paint, paintbrush

Materials
A small cup of water
Incense stick or toothpick

Cost: $5–$20. When it comes to the decorations of the spiral, the craft can get costly depending on how much you spend. If you are on a budget, stick with what you already have on hand, or you can buy crystal chips, stone beads, and shells from hobby stores. Gesso and acrylic paints can be bought in small bottles for this craft.

Time spent: 20 minutes to make the spiral incense holder, and 24 hours for it to dry

Instructions

Create sacred space to work in according to your path. Take a ball of air-dry clay large enough to fit in the palm of your hand. Roll the ball between your hands, shaping it into a long tube resembling a spaghetti noodle or a worm. Roll it out about twenty inches long.

Starting from one end, begin to roll the tube up into a spiral shape. Continue to roll until you've reached the other end. If cracks form in the clay, wet your finger with some water to smooth them out.

Decorate your spiral, if you wish, by pressing stones, crystals, shells, or other items into the spiral. Leave the center clear, as this is where you'll poke the hole for your incense.

Using a toothpick or the wooden end of an incense stick, poke a hole into the center of the spiral. Go all the way through the clay. Leave the toothpick or stick in the clay until it dries.

Set the incense holder to the side where it can dry. Give it at least twenty-four hours to dry thoroughly. Once it has dried, if you want to paint your incense holder, start with a thin coat of gesso paint. This seals the clay so that the acrylic paints don't soak into it and weaken your work. Let the gesso dry and then paint it with the acrylics. Choose colors like yellow, green, or brown, which are associated with Imbolc. When painting with the gesso and acrylic paints, make sure not to cover the hole at the center of the incense holder. You can keep the toothpick or incense stick in the hole until the paint dries to ensure that it doesn't get filled in.

Once everything is dry, you can use your incense holder. Light your incense stick and place it in the holder at the center. The ash will fall on the spiral. You can then dump the ash after the incense has burned down.

Spiral Offering Bowl

You can alter the above craft to make an offering bowl for your altar. These types of spiral dishes, called *coiled bowls*, were some of the earliest types of bowls made. This craft is so easy you can make it with your children, allowing you to have a discussion about Imbolc, the spiral, and what it means to be a Pagan or a witch.

Materials
White air-dry clay
Optional: gesso, acrylic paints

Tool
A small cup of water

Cost: $5–$20

Time spent: 20 minutes to make the spiral offering bowl, and 24 hours for it to dry

Instructions

Create sacred space to work in according to your path. Take a ball of air-dry clay about the size of your fist. Roll the ball between your hands, shaping it into a long tube resembling a spaghetti noodle or a worm. Make the tube about ¼ inch thick.

Starting from one end, begin to roll the tube up into a spiral shape. Continue to roll until you've reached the other end. If cracks form in the clay, wet your finger with some water to smooth them out.

As you are spiraling, curve up, making the walls of the bowl. You can use a wet finger to help "glue" the clay together as you spiral it up.

Set the bowl to the side where it can dry and give it at least twenty-four hours to dry thoroughly. Once it has dried, if you want to paint your bowl, start with a thin coat of gesso paint. This seals the clay so that the acrylic paints don't soak into it and weaken your work. Let the gesso dry and then paint it with the acrylics. Choose colors like yellow, green, or brown, which are associated with Imbolc.

Imbolc Meditations

Elizabeth Barrette

IMBOLC SPARKS THE FIRST beginning of spring, but outside it's still winter. Meditations in this season should be comfortable for indoors. Gather the energy from the resting season as you look within for that first spark of new life and new ideas. This is what you will nurture later in the warming season.

Breathing Meditations

Breath is the root of life. As such, breath work underlies many forms of meditation. It appears in traditions around the world. It can be used for diverse purposes. Mindful breathing can bring calm and promote healthy sleep. It can also awaken and invigorate the mind, body, and spirit. Learning to breathe properly opens a doorway to meditation as a practice.

Mindfulness of Breath Meditation

The most basic form is mindfulness of breath. This meditation quiets the "monkey mind" by giving it a task to focus on: paying attention to breathing. First, sit in a comfortable position. The traditional position is cross-legged on the floor or a meditation cushion, but sitting in a chair also works. The important part is to stay upright and relaxed. You may close your eyes or leave them open and focus softly on the floor just in front of you.

Note the environment around you. Remain aware of it without concentrating on it. As you breathe in, turn your attention to your breath. When your lungs are full, hold for a moment at that point and notice where you are in the cycle. As you breathe out, keep your attention on your breath. When your lungs are empty, hold for a moment at that point and notice where you are in the cycle. Breathe calmly but naturally, and hold your focus as best you can.

Especially in the beginning, it is common for mental chatter to distract you from your meditation. That's okay. When these thoughts come up, acknowledge them and gently set them aside. Return your attention to your breath. No matter what it is, it's not as important as breathing. Avoid criticizing yourself. Thoughts are not good or bad; they just are. You don't need them while you are meditating, so let them go. By deliberately focusing on your breath, your mind will learn to calm down and relax. Over time, you will come to associate meditation with inner peace, and your thoughts will become quieter sooner. Only the mindfulness of breath will remain.

Deep Breathing Meditation

Closely related to this is deep breathing for calm. Shallow chest breathing relates to stress and anxiety. Deep belly breathing relates to calm and relaxation. You can do this meditation anywhere, and it's often done in the midst of everyday life to lower stress. You may sit on the floor or in a chair, but you can also lie down on your back for this one.

Place one hand on your chest and the other hand on your belly. Breathe in, slow and deep. Your chest should barely move, while your belly should rise as your lungs inflate. Then breathe out, emptying your lungs as much as possible. Again, your chest should barely move, while your belly should sink as your lungs deflate.

Focus on your breath. Make it as slow and deep as you can. Feel the air moving through your body, in and out. As you slow your breathing, your heartbeat should follow. Slowing your body like this helps your mind relax too. As always, if distracting thoughts occur, simply acknowledge them and set them aside. They aren't important in this moment. Return your attention to your breath and keep going.

Loving-Kindness Meditation

This meditation, also known as *metta meditation*, is about developing compassion. This begins with self-compassion and moves through stages to encompass all beings. It improves concentration and mental focus. Practitioners sleep better, awake refreshed, and avoid nightmares. It promotes positive relationships with other people, animals, and higher powers. It supports a peaceful death, free of pain and fear; it can lead to a pleasant rebirth or to enlightenment.

Loving-kindness prayers, mantras, and meditations exist in many forms. These generally amount to a list of well-wishes for self and others, often followed by a commitment to help others. It is customary to switch the subject (e.g., "all beings") when going through the stages: first the self ("May I..."), then a loved one ("May [he/she/they]..."), then a neutral person ("May [he/she/they]..."), then a difficult person ("May [he/she/they]..."), and, finally, everyone ("May all beings everywhere..."). Here are multiple examples:

May all beings everywhere be happy and free.

May all beings everywhere be relieved of suffering and constraints.

May all beings everywhere live in equanimity, without attachment or anger.

May all beings everywhere awaken to their true nature and unity with all that is.

May the thoughts, words, and actions of my own life contribute in some way to the happiness, freedom, and awakening of all.

Begin by sitting comfortably. Become aware of your environment, your body, and your breath. Establish a stable foundation of existence within the here and now. Next, imagine yourself surrounded by unconditional love. Feel the warmth of this affection and acceptance flowing through you. Say the loving-kindness mantra "May I..." At first, you may not feel worthy or deserving of love. That's okay; it's common. It's also irrelevant. Love isn't earned; it's given. Everyone deserves love, especially self-love and self-compassion. Strive to treat yourself with kindness.

In the second stage, think of a friend or relative you love. Imagine this person surrounded by unconditional love. Visualize all the barriers to their safety and happiness melting away. Concentrate on your relationship and the joy it brings to both of you when you come together. Then say the loving-kindness mantra "May [he/she/they]..."

In the third stage, think of someone neutral, even someone you don't know personally. You might focus on the workers at a store or people who live in a distant town or country. Imagine them wrapped in the same unconditional love. You don't know their particular challenges, so just visualize all their problems dissolving away. Consider what a nice world it is when everyone thinks kindly of each other. Then say the loving-kindness mantra "May [he/she/they]..."

In the fourth stage, think of someone you don't get along with. They, too, deserve peace and freedom. Imagine them surrounded by unconditional love and the nastiness disappearing. There is no more strife. Then say the loving-kindness mantra "May [he/she/they]..."

In the fifth stage, extend the loving-kindness to everyone. Embrace all creatures with unconditional love. Then say the loving-kindness mantra "May all beings everywhere..."

Meditating daily, or even a few times each week, contributes to health and happiness. If you like the breath and loving-kindness meditations, you may wish to explore others later.

Imbolc Ritual

Sara Mellas

Chiaroscuro is an Italian term used to describe an artistic technique of using bold contrasts between light and dark to create volume in visual works. Its effects are distinct, impactful, and often dramatic. Metaphorically speaking, the use of chiaroscuro is a way of bringing things to life.

With Imbolc marking the halfway point between the dark days of the winter solstice and the lighter days of the spring equinox, it is an ideal time to meditate on what in our own lives we've been keeping in the dark—what we'd like to shed more light on, or what needs to be brought to light.

This visualization meditation employs the "dark" and "light" principles of chiaroscuro. It is used to first reveal truths and desires that have been suppressed or kept in the unconscious mind, then to align our energy with these truths of the soul and desires of the heart.

Depending on your meditation preferences, you may like to record yourself speaking the following text and perform it as a guided meditation. You may choose to speak the quoted phrases out loud or to think them silently.

Chiaroscuro Meditation

Situate yourself in a quiet indoor space away from any other people or distractions. Make sure the lights are turned off. Sit or recline in a position that feels comfortable to you.

The Dark

Slowly, inhale through your nose for four counts, then exhale for six counts. Repeat ten times, letting any thoughts that may arise pass on through. Keep returning your attention to your breath.
Release your counting and continue to breathe naturally.

In your mind's eye, visualize yourself standing before the entrance to a wooded forest. As you take in the expanse of tall trees, you notice an opening that appears to lead to a walking trail. You begin taking steps down this trail, into the forest.

As you walk, feeling the cool earth beneath your feet, the light grows dim behind the tree branches. Listen for any sounds. Do you hear leaves crunching? Is there a light swoosh from the wind? Are there birds or animals calling out?

Now, as you're deep into the forest, you notice a small circular fence to the side of the walking trail. You stop and discover that the fence encircles an opening to a subterranean cave. As you approach, you see a staircase carved into the earth, leading down into the cave.

One step at a time, you descend into the cave. The sounds you were hearing begin to fade, and the dim forest light gives way to complete darkness. As you continue down the staircase, you repeat the phrase "I am safe in the dark" three times.

You come to the bottom of the staircase and take a seat on the floor of the cave. The dark, soundless stillness provides an environment of total calm. Take three deep breaths through your nose, allowing yourself to be fully present in the cave.

When you are fully at ease, ask the question, "What have I been keeping in the dark?" Breathe slowly and wait for a response; you may hear the answer with your inner ear or see a visual in your mind's eye. Notice what comes up without judgment and sit with it for several rounds of breath.

When you are ready, ask the next question: "What does my soul want to bring into the light?" Continue breathing as you wait for an answer as before.

Return your awareness to the cave and pose one final question: "Am I ready to call in the light?" Breathe steadily, noticing any resistance or sensations that may arise. Continue breathing through these for as long as you need, until you feel yourself answer an honest yes.

The Light

Feel yourself fully in the darkness of your visualization, focusing on the thing your soul wants to bring into the light. Imagine this thing taking on a physical form. What size is it? Shape? Color? Material? Does it move or stay still? Hold this image in your awareness, feeling its energy before you in the shadows of the cave.

With the permission from your inner authority, affirm, "I now call in the light." Take a deep breath.

From the opening of the cave through which you descended the stairs, a ray of golden light pours down into the cave, illuminating the space above and around you. Feel the light as it meets the crown of your head, then washes over your neck, shoulders, torso, hands, hips, legs, and feet. You are now fully immersed in the soft glow of golden light.

Bring your attention to the center of your chest. With each exhale, see the golden light start to expand from your heart center, shining over more and more of the area around you. Continue breathing as the light reaches toward the physical manifestation of the thing your soul wants to bring into the light. Observe as the golden light meets it, wrapping it in the same soft glow that you yourself are sitting in.

Take in every physical detail of the thing illuminated before you, the entirety of the surrounding cave awash in gold. Recognize it as a part of you, connected by light to your heart space. Repeat three times, "I am safe in the light."

Visualize the distance between you and the thing diminishing, coming closer and closer toward you. When it is near enough to reach out and touch, release the visual of its physical form, allowing it to become pure energy. Then, feel this energy become one with yours.

Affirm, "I am light." You stand up and begin to ascend the staircase, each step now clearly visible. You reach the opening of the cave, and sunlight pours through the forest trees. Say once again, "I am light."

You return to the walking trail and begin moving back toward the entrance of the forest, golden light illuminating your path. You reach the start of the trail and emerge from the thick of trees, saying for a final time, "I am light."

Slowly, open your eyes. Take several deep breaths before moving or standing. Your meditation is now complete.

Candle Ritual

From here, you can perform a simple candle ritual to deepen your practice. Any candle may be used, but to further support your intention, use a spell-size candle in the color that best aligns with the nature of what you brought into the light during your meditation.

- White: Renewal, peace, cleansing, freedom
- Black: Protection, severance, transformation, magic
- Red: Strength, passion, motivation, perseverance
- Orange: Energy, creativity, attraction, success
- Yellow: Confidence, joy, personal power, adventure
- Green: Healing, abundance, relationships, luck, generosity
- Blue: Communication, truth, serenity, clear thinking
- Purple: Divine guidance, intuition, spirituality, sovereignty
- Pink: Unconditional love, self-love, compassion, kindness

Recall the physical image in your mind's eye, then light the candle, saying out loud, "I am light." Let the candle burn down fully, celebrating what your soul will no longer keep in the dark.

Notes

Notes

Ostara

The Challenges of Ostara

Lupa

AH, SPRING—THE TIME WHEN winter's chill subsides and we anticipate the arrival of flowers, sunshine, and cute baby animals. The arrival of the spring equinox in the Northern Hemisphere often brings with it associations of gentleness and ease—but there's another side to this sabbat. Every time of year presents its challenges, and Ostara is no exception.

Samhain is the sabbat most associated with death and darkness, though Yule also brings us the longest night and the desire to survive until the return of the sun. They mark seasons in which life in the Northern Hemisphere is often at its most taxed, with cold temperatures and scarce food culling many from deer herds and wolf packs alike. But nature always presents dangers, and death may strike at any time of the year, even when things seem warmest and sunniest.

Seasonal Strain

First, consider that conditions in one part of the Northern Hemisphere will be different from those elsewhere. Ostara in the southern United States may be full of wildflowers, but in the Arctic Circle, it's still cold with plenty of ice and snow. Even places in the same area but at different elevations will have significant variations in temperature and signs of life; where the top of a mountain may seem lifeless and frozen, the foothills could be seeing the first greening of the year.

Speaking of green, the flush of new growth from plants symbolizes hope after winter's dormancy. And to be sure, there are plenty of herbivorous animals that are able to make the most of newly sprouted grass and other foliage. But the growth may not be fast enough to meet demand, especially if chilly temperatures hinder the plants' return. For some, the arrival of sweet new leaves may be weeks or months away.

Think of those animals that rely on berries or nuts for the majority of their annual calories and stash them for consumption over the winter. By the equinox, their stores may be lean indeed or completely depleted, with no hope of replenishment anytime soon. Even in the comparatively mild areas of the Pacific Northwest, for example, the earliest berries to ripen are salmonberries (*Rubus spectabilis*). However, they won't be available in abundance until late May or early June. Late cold snaps can kill off early-emerging insects, leaving birds and other predators with a shortfall of food.

This means that ongoing hunger is very much a part of Ostara. In fact, for some species, this is one of the riskiest times of year because their main food sources aren't yet available. And if we consider that the Wheel of the Year is based on Western European agrarian cycles, Ostara could be similarly dangerous for subsistence farmers if they had already eaten their winter stores and conditions did not allow early, fast-growing crops to mature early enough.

For most modern Western Pagans, the ebbs and flows of agriculture are abstract and theoretical at best. I can walk into any of over a dozen grocery stores within less than an hour's drive from my home and get a wide variety of fresh produce year-round, along with meat, seafood, cheese, and other staples. Of those who have vegetable gardens, a bad year may mean humorous photos of a small handful of anemic cherry tomatoes and a pathetic little carrot or two but no serious danger to our food security.

But Ostara reminds me of the times when I've run through my money days before my next paycheck drops. It's the moments when an unexpected expense chews through my reserves. And while the grocery stores may be full of food, sometimes I'm not able to bring home as much as I'd like. So while I may not have lived through a widespread famine, I've experienced my own times of scarcity.

The Mortality of Youth

Ostara represents the first fertility of the year. By this point, the first young animals have been born; bear cubs emerge from dens with their mothers, and insect eggs that have overwintered in sheltered places start to hatch as the temperatures rise. Deer, many heavily pregnant, eagerly devour the sweet new grass shoots after a winter of dried leaves and tree bark, while ephemeral spring wildflowers unfurl through the lengthening days. The fruiting bodies of some fungi, such as certain oyster mushrooms and wood ears, often emerge by the time the equinox dawns to spread their spores across the land. After a long, bleak winter, every bit of color and new growth is a welcome sight.

With all that life in evidence, it's easy to forget that death is ever-present. You've probably heard the expression "breeding like rabbits." Rabbits and hares are symbols of fertility because they have such large litters of young, and often more than one litter a year. The eastern cottontail rabbit, for example, may reach sexual maturity at two months of age, and in some cases, a female may reproduce in her first year. She can have up to seven litters a year in warmer regions, and a single litter might have up to twelve kits.

It's not just lagomorphs that are so fecund, though. Rodents also have multiple large litters a year. Many songbirds will raise two or three clutches of young between their spring and fall migrations. And even some animals that only breed once every year or two may still produce many young in one batch: hawksbill sea turtles lay more than one hundred eggs in each nest, while a Chinook salmon will bury thousands of eggs in streambed gravel during her one and only breeding season, after which she dies within a few days.

It is not only the spring Chinook who experience mortality during the season of Ostara. The reason so many animals produce large numbers of young is that most will not survive to adulthood. Over half of all fawns won't see their second spring, and the numbers are similar for baby rabbits, mice, and birds. If 1 percent of a sea turtle's eggs become adults, that's a pretty good success rate. Of the salmon fry that successfully hatch, most won't survive their round trip to the ocean and then back to their birthplace to breed.

What's with all the infant mortality among wildlife? Every living being has something that will eat it, and young animals are especially vulnerable because they haven't developed their adult defenses yet. They're small and weak and generally slower or less armored than their parents, making them easier targets for hungry predators. And, of course, young animals are not immune to diseases, nor are they safe from life-threatening injuries. A child with a broken arm will be taken to a hospital for a cast and heal up just fine, but a fledgling bird with a broken wing is likely to die of starvation or predation. *Bambi* may be a beloved animated film with adorable baby animals in an idyllic forest, but it's hardly a documentary (and it removes many of the natural and human dangers that author Felix Salten included in the books the movie was based on).

So what's actually happening to Bambi and his buddies? Well, nature doesn't waste nutrients, and one animal's death means another's life. It's not just birds and bunnies raising young during Ostara. Foxes, wolves, weasels, and other predatory animals also have hungry little mouths to feed and growing families to tend to. Even if a fawn were to die of a congenital defect rather than predation, it would almost certainly end up as food anyway. The line between predator and scavenger is almost nonexistent, as most carnivorous and omnivorous animals will both hunt live prey and take advantage of convenient carcasses to survive.

Even with successes, many of those meat-eating youngsters won't live through their first year either. Some never make it out of the den for reasons ranging from stillbirth to starvation; others meet a sad end in the jaws of larger predators or die from accidents or infections. Ostara is a time of hope that new lives will replenish the world, but some of those lives must end prematurely in order to strengthen the chances that others will thrive.

No Gentle Animals

With all this death and catatrophe, you might be feeling bad for all those poor little deer and bunnies falling helplessly before the onslaught of vicious predators. Nothing could be further from the truth. The "nice," "gentle" animals we often associate with the flowery festivities of Ostara are often able to give their rivals a run for their money—or at least put up a good fight.

It's true that many prey animals rely on running, hiding, or both for their primary defense. Deer, rabbits, and antelope are among the long-legged creatures able to flee danger at high speed. This allows them to outrun predators that are primarily sprinters, though persistence predators may be able to wear their prey down over time even if they can't achieve the high speeds of their quarry.

If dangerous animals can't find you, they can't harm you, and this strategy works well for animals ranging from cephalopods to rodents and more. *Countershading*, in which the upper parts of an animal are dark while the underside is light, gives a wide range of animals an edge in blending in with their environment by flattening. Think of a mouse with a brown back and white belly, for example. The darker topside makes it more difficult to see from above if it's running through dry grass, but if it's climbing in a bush, a predator below would be less likely to see its white belly against the light shining through.

Many songbirds, particularly the females of the species, have plumage in earth-toned patterns that allow them to stay camouflaged while sitting on a nest of eggs, even as their male counterparts may draw attention to themselves with bright colors and songs. Cuttlefish are well-known for their exceptional ability to change not only their color but texture as well to blend in seamlessly with a wide variety of habitats and backgrounds; even when confronted with artificial patterns in laboratory settings, they are remarkably adept at imitating stripes and checkerboards.

So far, I've talked about passive defenses. But what happens if these don't work? Even the most seemingly harmless creature can be surprisingly fierce when cornered or captured.

Rabbits and hares, of course, are the animals most associated with Ostara for their fertility. But they're hardly helpless in a fight, at least against a similarly sized predator. Those strong back legs that allow them to accelerate quickly can also deliver a dangerous kick. Not only do these lagomorphs do battle against each other during breeding season, but they can deter, injure, or even kill a smaller predator with a well-aimed blow. They're also capable of delivering a nasty bite with their sharp, chisel-like incisors. If you want children's literature that has a more realistic portrayal of rabbits, skip *Bambi* and pick up Richard Adams's *Watership Down*; while rabbits do not have quite as military a hierarchy as depicted, the violence between rabbits is not entirely unrealistic.

In the same vein, deer shouldn't be underestimated. More than one hapless human has found themselves at the business end of hard, pointy antlers during the annual rut. A white-tailed deer may not be as large as its cousin the moose, but more than one death can be attributed to angry bucks goring hapless hunters or wildlife viewers. A deer doesn't need antlers to be dangerous either; those hooves are sharp! Deer can kick with both front and hind legs, and there's a real danger of getting trampled to the point of injury or death, whether from a 120-pound white-tailed doe or an 800-pound cow moose. Trying to make friends with your cervine neighbors by feeding them only increases your risk of injury, as deer that have lost their fear of humans are more likely to attack, not less.

I've mostly been talking about wild animals, but sheep often get wrapped into Ostara symbolism, along with their fertile role during Imbolc. Lambs are especially associated with the season, and having helped to raise numerous generations of sheep, I can confirm that a young lamb is a pretty benign, helpless little being. Not so the ewes and rams though. Adults of both sexes can do serious damage with a firm head-butt, even if they lack horns. They're a danger not only to legitimate predators but to well-meaning humans trying to give aid to a newborn lamb. (I speak from experience!)

Fire is what burns in the heart of every cell of every living being; we all carry its heat within us. And although a particular animal may seem sedate, nature's many intricate relationships require that even the meekest must sometimes pull forth the fire within to defend themselves.

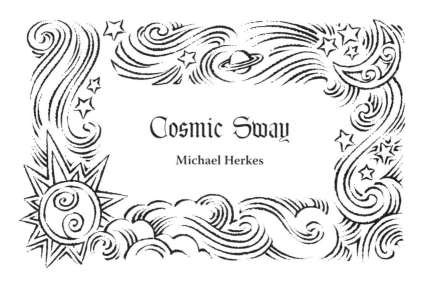

Cosmic Sway

Michael Herkes

As the Wheel of the Year turns, we find ourselves approaching Ostara, that magical time when winter's grip finally loosens and spring bursts forth in all its glory. This is a season of renewal, balance, and fresh beginnings. Let's dive into the energies at play and explore some meaningful ways to celebrate.

Observing Ostara

Ostara, falling on the spring equinox around March 20, marks the moment when day and night stand in perfect equilibrium. It's as if the whole world takes a deep breath, pausing before the rush of spring's growth. This balance offers us a unique opportunity to reflect on our own lives—where are we in harmony, and where might we need to make adjustments?

The energy of Ostara is all about potential. Think of a seed still nestled in the earth but vibrating with the possibility of what it might become. That's the kind of magic we're working with here. It's a time to plant intentions, both literally and metaphorically. Many witches choose to start their herb gardens now, infusing each seed with their hopes for the coming season.

One of my favorite Ostara rituals involves eggs. Yeah, I know, it sounds a bit cliché, but hear me out. Eggs are these perfect little symbols of potential. Take a raw egg and carefully blow out the contents (save them for cooking later!). Now you've got this delicate shell—a blank canvas. Decorate it however you like: paint, glitter, herbs stuck on with glue—whatever feels right to you. However, I recommend choosing materials that are eco-friendly. As you work, focus on what you want to bring into your life. When you're done, find a special spot in your garden or a pot of earth and bury it. You're planting your intentions, letting them germinate in the fertile spring soil.

Now, let's talk about the start of Aries season on March 20. Aries energy is like a jolt of caffeine after the dreamy vibes of Pisces. It's bold, it's brash, and it's ready to charge headfirst into new adventures. This is fantastic energy for kicking off new projects or finally tackling that thing you've been putting off. Light a red candle, grab your favorite fiery crystals like carnelian or sunstone, and make a list of all the awesome stuff you're going to accomplish. Don't hold back—Aries energy is all about dreaming big.

April Moon Magic

Fresh out of the gate, April 1 brings us a Full Moon in Libra at 10:12 p.m. Now, Libra is all about balance (sensing a theme here?), but it's also about relationships and beauty. This is a perfect time for some serious self-love magic. Draw yourself a bath and add some rose petals and a few drops of your favorite essential oil premixed with a carrier oil. As you soak, really feel into all the things you love about yourself. Maybe even write them down afterward. This Full Moon is also great for smoothing over any rough patches in your relationships. Consider doing a small ritual to send healing energy to any connections that need it.

Mid-month, on April 17 at 7:52 a.m., we've got a New Moon in Aries. Remember that bold Aries energy we talked about? Well, it's back and supercharged by the New Moon's potential. This is prime manifesting time, folks. Write down your biggest, wildest dreams. Don't censor yourself. Then burn the paper, releasing those intentions to the universe. Just be careful—Aries energy can be a bit impulsive, so maybe sleep on any big decisions for a day or two.

Earth Day

Rounding out our magical month, we've got Earth Day on April 22. As witches and Pagans, our connection to the earth is central to our practice. This is a day to really honor that relationship. Spend some time outside, feet bare on the ground if you can. Listen to the birds, feel the breeze, really connect with the world around you. Maybe do a cleanup of a local park or beach or start a compost bin. Whatever you do, approach it as an act of devotion to the earth that sustains us all.

Summary

Throughout this season, pay attention to the signs of spring emerging around you. Notice the first buds on the trees, the return of birdsong in the morning, the way the air starts to smell different. These aren't just nice things to observe—they're messages from the world around us, reminding us that we too are part of this cycle of renewal.

One of my favorite ways to tap into spring energy is to forage for early greens. Dandelion leaves, chickweed, and wild garlic are often among the first to appear. Learning to identify and use these plants connects us deeply to the seasons and the land we live on. Just make sure you're foraging responsibly and safely!

As we move through this season of growth and renewal, remember that magic isn't just about spells and rituals. It's about living in harmony with the energies around us, about being fully present in each moment. The real magic happens when we align ourselves with the rhythms of the natural world.

With that said, this springtime, I encourage you to step outside. Feel the Sun on your face. Dig your hands into the earth. Plant something—a seed, an intention, a dream. Watch it grow. Nurture it. And know that you too are growing, changing, renewing with each turn of the wheel. As we embrace this season of new beginnings, may your magic be strong, your heart be light, and your spirit be renewed. Blessed Ostara, and happy spring!

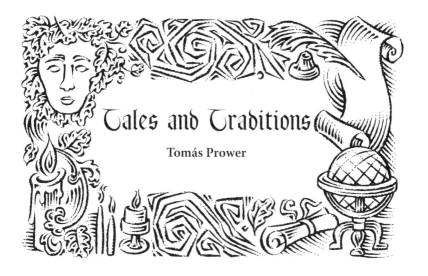

Tales and Traditions

Tomás Prower

OSTARA MARKS THE DAY of the vernal equinox, the time of the year when, amid the cosmic ballet of our solar system, planet earth receives equal time of day and night due to the way the sun's rays reach our sphere. Moreover, it is a time of growing optimism because from today until the autumnal equinox six months from now, the days will be longer than the nights. However, we're not in the full bosom of warmth and bloom just yet, as winter coldness tends to still linger, balancing between the heat and the cold, the future and the past. Balance is not only the way of Ostara; it's also the way of nature, the way of the world, and it is also the way of heaven and the gods if they be wise and benevolent. By achieving balance in our own lives, perhaps we, too, can be more like the Divine.

Erinle: A Better You Through Balance

Among the Yoruba peoples who live in West Africa, largely in what is now Nigeria, there is belief in a wise deity who embodies the balance of both nature and human nature. Their deities are called *Orishas*, and this particular Orisha's name is Erinle, a dual-gendered divinity who can transform into male or female as they wish. Depending upon their gender of the moment, they hold sacred patronage over different dominions.

As a male, Erinle is primarily the Orisha of hunting and healing, which includes both physical strength and athleticism as well as medicine. So great is his knowledge of medicine in particular, he acts as chief physician to the Orishas. However, this knowledge of medicine comes from his ability to balance his masculinity and femininity—seeing, knowing, and interacting with the world from two completely different perspectives. And those different perspectives add to a greater whole of knowledge and wisdom. This is especially apt for the healing arts, wherein life and death are matters of degree and balance. Medicine can be poison if not taken at the right dosage just as much as fortitude in exercising can be folly if the body doesn't get rest and recovery. Erinle's understanding of this balance in all things allows them to be such a celebrated doctor.

As a female, Erinle is the Orisha of the waters, especially the life-giving waters of the rivers, which nourish the land and quench the thirst of humans and animals alike. So, too, does knowledge of balance allow Erinle to properly steward the great responsibility of the waters of life. Not enough, and the land withers and the people die. Too much, and the land floods and the crops are equally ruined. Move too swiftly, and it can cause great danger to life and property. Move too slowly, and the water stagnates and becomes putrid. Water that just focuses on itself can do as it pleases, leaving the world around it to suffer as an effect. However, water that understands the world outside of itself, the terrestrial world, can better work in tandem with it and be revered for it. Erinle's understanding of the balance of all things allows her to be such a wise steward of this most essential resource to all life on earth.

Thus it is with us and the lesson of balance that the Ostara equinox teaches. In order to live a more enriched life, we need to have a more holistic worldview. Being able to see different points of view, to walk a mile in someone else's shoes, and to understand the ripple effects that our choices and actions have on other people and the environment allows us to be of better help to those who need us. Too often, we suffer from a blinding myopia. We learn and study that which we only want to know, speak only to those who would agree with us, and exist in an echo chamber of self-selected social media groups and info sources that don't challenge us, don't offer anything radically new into our comfy world of crippling contentment.

But being uncomfortable is where all growth lies, both physical and spiritual. Your muscles won't grow if you don't keep lifting progressively heavier weight. Your endurance to travel and move farther for longer doesn't increase if you never push yourself past your farthest distance. Likewise, you can't learn a new skill such as an instrument, a language, or a craft if you're not willing to experience the uncomfortableness of being a novice, making mistakes, and sometimes looking like a fool. To expand your magic, your relationship with the Divine, and your understanding of life and spirit around you, you need to be okay with being uncomfortable. You have to be willing to be confused at times or, most painfully, accept that you were possibly wrong and that some of your deepest-held beliefs neither serve you nor advance you, even if they once did long ago.

Erinle themselves is no stranger to this universal maxim of "growth lies outside your comfort zone." Even though an Orisha, they gained much wisdom and knowledge of balance the hard way, most infamously in their romantic relationship with Oshun, the Orisha of, among other things, love, luxury, beauty, and pleasure. Oshun fell in love with how Erinle understood the nuances and needs of a woman because Erinle could be a woman and thus understand their female spouse on a level no male could. Nevertheless, Erinle's dedication to balance in their life compelled them to live half the year with Oshun and half the year with their male friends. Oshun, however, was not happy with having to share Erinle's attentions for such a long stretch of time every year, and so their life together broke down. Oshun left Erinle to raise their children as a single parent. Thus, through this pain, Erinle learned that balance in all things must be tempered by the knowledge that all our choices have consequences for those around us.

And so, this Ostara, as the daylight begins to get longer, take the seasonal lesson and Erinle's wisdom to heart. Be not stiff and uncompromising, and neither surround yourself in an echo chamber nor prevent yourself from growing just because it involves discomfort. A balance in all things is the wisest course. Yet always keep in mind that sometimes balance isn't a perfect divide, but rather a give-and-take compromise.

Feasts and Treats

Nathan M. Hall

THE SPRING EQUINOX STARTS the cycle of gentle warming of the land. In more temperate areas, things like baby lettuces are beginning to sprout and chickens are beginning to lay eggs in abundance. This tart might be my favorite recipe at the moment. It's fun, fresh, and less heavy than a full-sized quiche.

Bacon and Cheese Quiche Tart

A tart pan helps to create a slightly less-decadent quiche than the full size but still offers a satisfying amount, especially when paired with the Field Greens Salad on page 147.

Prep time: 25 minutes
Cooking time: 25–30 minutes
Servings: 6–8

Crust

1½ cups flour

½ teaspoon sea salt

1½ sticks unsalted butter (about 12 tablespoons) cut into small cubes and kept in the refrigerator until ready to use

2–3 tablespoons ice water

Filling

½ package of bacon, fried crisp and crumbled

1 shallot, peeled and sliced thin

8 ounces baby bella, cremini, or white button mushrooms, cleaned and cut into quarters

4 ounces shredded cheese, Swiss or Gruyere recommended

4 eggs

1 cup half-and-half

Pinch of thyme

Pinch of nutmeg

You'll want a 9-inch tart pan for this recipe, the kind where the bottom of the pan pops out. Also, having pie weights or dried beans is a must for blind baking.

Preheat oven to 375°F.

For the crust, using a food processor, mix together the flour and sea salt. Still using the food processor, add in the cubes of butter bit by bit, pulsing as you go until it has formed into a crumbly, pea-sized mix. Add the water one tablespoon at a time and continue pulsing until the dough has just come together. We don't want to overwork or overwater it, so as long as our dough is mostly together, you can grab whatever stragglers are still in the food processor and add them to the main dough ball. Form the dough into a thick disc, something easy to roll out later, and wrap it in plastic wrap. If you take your rolling pin and give it a few rolls while it's wrapped in the plastic, it will be easier to remove later. You can let the dough rest in the fridge for up to a couple days like this.

When you're ready, flour a surface, remove the plastic wrap, and use a rolling pin to roll the dough out until it's a disc that's just larger than the size of your tart pan. Sometimes I do this on parchment paper to make it easier for me to lift and manipulate the dough.

Gently lift and position the dough into the tart pan (flipping and setting aside the parchment paper if you used it). Make sure to tuck down as much of the dough as you can to remove air pockets, and trim off any excess dough that's hanging over.

Blind bake by placing a piece of parchment paper on top of the dough in the tart pan and filling with the pie weights or dried beans. Place in the oven for 12 minutes.

When done, remove from the oven and allow to cool. The pie weights or beans will be hot, so I usually leave them in while I start the filling and remove them when they're safe to touch.

For the filling, after you've cooked the bacon, use a paper towel to wipe up most of the grease and then fry the shallot for 2–3 minutes before adding the mushrooms. Sweat the mushrooms in the pan until most of the excess moisture has evaporated. Remove from heat and combine with the bacon. Take the bacon, mushroom, and shallot mix and spoon into the bottom of the quiche crust. Top with the shredded cheese.

Crack open the eggs and whisk together with the half-and-half, thyme, and nutmeg until well incorporated. Pour the egg mix over the top of the ingredients in the quiche crust, filling almost to the top.

Bake for 25–30 minutes and remove when the egg has just set. If it's jiggly when you nudge it, leave it in for a few more minutes.

Remove from the oven and let rest for 15–20 minutes. When you're ready, set the tart pan on top of a bowl and very gingerly release the ring from the pan. You can now slide it off the pan bottom onto a serving dish. There won't be leftovers, but if somehow you can resist, keep them covered in the fridge for up to two days.

Field Greens Salad

This simple salad is a staple in my household. If you have a Mason-style jar with a lid, it makes quick work of the homemade dressing.

Prep time: 10–15 minutes
Servings: 4–6

½ shallot clove, minced
2–3 tablespoons red wine vinegar
4 tablespoons olive oil
1 teaspoon French mustard (Maille recommended)
½ teaspoon Italian seasoning or Herbes de Provence

Pinch of fresh ground black pepper

1 teaspoon sea salt, more to taste

1 bag mixed greens, or make your own with a mix of young and tender spinach, arugula, lettuces, chard, or any other delicious edible green

In a bowl or Mason jar, place the minced shallot and red wine vinegar. Let sit for about 10–15 minutes to help mellow out the bite of the raw shallot. When ready, drop in the olive oil, mustard, seasonings, black pepper, and sea salt. Stir vigorously with a fork, or if using the jar, just put the lid on and shake until it's well incorporated. Give it a taste, and if it's still got too much of a kick, add some more salt to smooth out the flavors.

Chop up your greens and put in a bowl (or empty the bag) and mix together with the dressing just before you're ready to serve. Because these greens are so tender, they quickly get mushy, so don't feel like you need to bring it to the table ready to eat.

Strawberry Pretzel Salad

Fresh strawberries are pretty much available year-round and make for a much tastier, less mushy version than using frozen.

Prep time: 20 minutes

Prep time: 12 minutes

Prep time: 2 hours or overnight

Servings: 8–12

½ cup melted butter

1¼ cups pretzel sticks, crushed

½ cup granulated sugar

½ cup water, plus 1 cup cold water

Ice cubes

6-ounce package strawberry gelatin or gelatin alternative

2 pounds strawberries, hulled and cut in half (Slice if you have larger strawberries.)

1 cup heavy whipping cream
¼ cup confectioners' sugar, plus another ½ cup
8 ounces cream cheese

Preheat oven to 350°F.

Melt butter in microwave at 5-second increments until it becomes a liquid. Combine crushed pretzels with granulated sugar and melted butter in a large bowl. Empty into a 9 × 13-inch glass baking dish and evenly distribute, pressing down firmly to compact.

Place in oven for 12 minutes and then remove and allow to completely cool.

While waiting on the crust, bring ½ cup water just to a boil and pour into a metal bowl. Add in the gelatin, stirring until dissolved, and then add the other 1 cup cold water with a few ice cubes. Stir until you see it beginning to set a little and then fish out the ice cubes. Add strawberries to the bowl and place in the refrigerator.

Now the clock's against you! But don't worry, we're going to make a whipped cream mixture that shouldn't take more than a few minutes to bring together. Don't take a break though, because if you wait too long, your gelatin will set in the bowl!

In a stand mixer, use the whisk attachment and pour the heavy whipping cream into the bowl. Start on the low setting and slowly increase to medium speed. When the cream starts to firm up, stop and add the ¼ cup confectioners' sugar. Start whisking again on a low setting and work up slowly to medium speed in order to prevent the sugar from poofing out of the bowl. When you start to see soft peaks, stop the mixer and add in the remaining ½ cup confectioners' sugar and the cream cheese. Gradually bring the mixer up to speed again and whisk for two minutes.

Using a rubber spatula, pour out the whipped cream and cream cheese mixture onto the cooled pretzel crust, smoothing out and making as even as possible without being too fussy.

Pull the gelatin and strawberry mix out of the refrigerator and give it a stir, breaking up any bits that have set, before pouring over your whipped cream. Smooth out the top and cover with plastic wrap, or a lid if you have one, and put in the refrigerator for at least 2 hours (overnight is safer) to allow gelatin to completely set.

When ready to serve, cut into 3 × 3 pieces for about 12 servings, or be bold and cut them into 4 × 3 pieces for 8 servings.

Crafty Crafts

Raechel Henderson

OSTARA MARKS THE BEGINNING of spring. The snow has receded to reveal the first greens of the season. These plants offer a welcome reprieve from the last of the winter stores in both nutrition and taste. Spring cleaning is the name of the game as we throw open our windows to clear out our homes of stagnant air and energy. We celebrate the sun's growing warmth, the renewal of the earth, and the promise of abundance and life that Ostara brings. Despite having been co-opted by Christianity, you can still see many of the early symbols in the bunnies, eggs, and baskets that form the backbone of Easter celebrations. Where Imbolc is the rebirth of the sun, Ostara is the rebirth of the earth. It is also a time of giving thanks for having survived the dark time of winter and emerging, blinking, into the light of spring.

Non-Salt Dough Offering Coins

When foraging or working with *genii locorum*—local land spirits—you might want to leave an offering. Some practices use water, smoke, or energy for offerings. But if you want to leave something else, you'll need to be careful that it won't have unintended consequences.

These offering coins are made from just three ingredients that won't harm the environment when you place them out in nature. Regular offerings can have a negative impact on local flora and fauna. Chocolate, bread, and milk can be dangerous for animals to ingest and can cause mold. The metals from coins can leach into the ground. These coins don't have salt, which can also harm the soil and the environment.

These coins can also be used on altars to replace food or drink offerings. Sometimes leaving food out isn't practical. Witches with ADHD might forget to dispose of it, or there might be pest problems. Putting aside a portion of food might not be possible if you live in a food-insecure household. These coins can be used as a substitute.

Magically speaking, cornstarch is associated with the element of earth and has properties of protection and luck. It is also good for binding energies into spellwork, or in this case, into the coins. Baking soda is also associated with the earth element and has magical properties of raising energy and protection. Both of these ingredients are useful in, first, binding your gratitude to the coins, and then, second, enhancing those feelings of gratitude. By mixing them with the water, baking them in the oven, and then allowing them to cool down, you are invoking all four elements to create these coins, further enhancing their magic.

This is a craft that you can do with friends and family, portioning the dough out to everyone so that they can make their own unique coins. With children you can talk about the importance of gratitude when working with the Divine, whether that be deities, helper spirits, or ancestors. When working with friends, you can take turns talking about what you are grateful for and how you'll be using these coins in the future.

Materials
½ cup cornstarch
1 cup baking soda
¾ cup water

Tools
Saucepan
Whisk
Stove and oven
Wooden spoon
Plastic wrap
Parchment paper
Baking sheet
Cooling rack
Optional: bread knife or toothpick
> *Cost:* $5
> *Time spent:* 1 hour or more

Instructions
Start by creating sacred space to work in according to your path. Mix the cornstarch and baking soda together in the saucepan. Use the whisk to ensure they are evenly mixed and there are no lumps. Next, add in the water, stirring to mix. The cornstarch and baking soda should be dissolved in the water.

Place the saucepan on the stove on medium-high heat. Stir the mixture with the wooden spoon until it has formed a dough. Remove it from the heat immediately and turn it out on a flat surface.

Knead the dough. Be careful, as it will be hot. Knead it until it has reached the consistency of dough. Form it into a ball and wrap it in plastic wrap so that it doesn't dry out as it continues to cool down. Wait five to ten minutes, then unwrap the dough and knead it again until it has a smooth texture.

Pull off small lumps of the dough about the size of your thumb. Roll them into balls and then flatten them. As you work the dough, think about what offering means to you. What would it look like for you to use these coins? What words would you say as you left them? In what circumstances would you use them? Thinking about this and planning it out ahead of time makes it more likely that you will use them in the future.

Leave the "coins" as is, or you can mark them with symbols, sigils, or runes, such as the rune Gebo, which means "gift." To do this, use the edge of a bread knife or toothpick. Choose symbols that resonate with you. You can also write words such as "thankful," "thanks," or "gift" on the coins.

Preheat the oven to the lowest setting, or 170°F. Place the coins onto a parchment-lined baking sheet. Bake them for forty-five minutes. Flip the coins halfway through the baking process. Remove them from the oven and let them cool on a cooling rack.

Store them in a tightly sealed container. Make sure they have cooled completely before you store them away. If they are still warm, condensation will occur in the container and can ruin your coins.

Take the coins out with you when you go foraging. As you take from a plant, tree, or the landscape, tell the land spirit of that place "thank you" and leave a coin as a representation of your gratitude. The coin will be broken down by the weather. When you use them on your altar, specifically state that they are coins to show your appreciation for all the help your ancestors, deities, and helper spirits have given you. They can be disposed of by burying them, washing them away in a stream or other body of water, or even flushed down the toilet.

Ostara Meditations

Elizabeth Barrette

OSTARA IS THE SEASON when new life springs forth with vigor. Meditations for this time should catch that energy and encourage you to get moving. Clear your mind so that you can channel your focus toward desired accomplishments. Get outside and enjoy the spring weather with mindful appreciation. You can do this with a manifestation meditation and moving meditations.

Manifestation Meditation

Manifestation differs from most other types of meditation because it is goal oriented. You use the state of "being" that the meditation creates to advance your plans for "doing." Your inner peace and mental focus become foundations for achieving what you want. Like other types, manifestation meditation reduces stress and anxiety, increases mental clarity, and creates a more positive outlook. This tends to improve your performance.

Because it works with your subconscious mind, manifestation meditation is best done right after you wake up or just before bed. You can do it lying down, but if that makes you fall asleep, sit up on the floor or in a chair. Meditating outside can also work well and connect you with nature.

Begin by focusing on your breath. Aim for a calm, relaxed state of mind. Cup your hands to receive blessings. Make your statement of intent, describing what you want to manifest. Attune yourself to the universe, which creates everything. Then say, "I manifest that which I desire." If you feel unworthy or uncertain, allow your doubts and fears to bubble up. Acknowledge them and set them aside.

Focus on your goal. Visualize the steps required to achieve it. Imagine yourself taking those steps. Consider the time frame that you have for this progress. Picture the goal in as much detail as you can. See yourself enjoying your accomplishments.

Now pull back a little and really focus on the next step in your project. Use all your senses to imagine yourself taking that step. What will you need to do, where, and when? How will you feel after you have done it? Return your attention to your breath, and end the current meditation on this note.

You will need to follow up with further sessions as you progress through your project. Set aside some time each day to dedicate to your goal. Begin every session with a few minutes of meditation. Each time, focus on the step that you plan to take today. Concentrate on your certainty that this is possible and you can do it. Believe in yourself. Then say, "I know that I can achieve my purpose. I believe deeply in myself. I see clearly how I attain my goals and aspirations. I feel a strong desire to manifest my goals. I put in the daily dedication that is required to make this progress. Every day takes me closer to my aspirations."

You also need to cultivate trust in yourself and the universe. Imagine that you have attained all that you desire. See yourself, as vividly as you can, having already met your goals. Visualize yourself in great detail after you have fulfilled your intentions. Where are you, what do you look like, and who are you talking with? The more details, the better. Then say, "I always believe in myself. I trust myself to complete these goals. I trust the loving energy of the universe to meet my needs. This is changing my life for the better." If you encounter setbacks, return to your meditation and shore up your manifestation energy. You can do it.

Moving Meditations

Whereas most types of meditation involve sitting still, moving meditations are all about finding peace through motion. This is also called a *flow state* or *being in the zone.* You are relaxed and alert at the same time. You move automatically, gracefully, without needing to think about or plan your moves. It allows you to unwind and exercise at the same time.

Many types of activity can work for moving meditation. Ideally, you want something that is repetitive so that you don't have to devote a lot of attention to following a complicated pattern. It should be just challenging enough to hold your attention. Allow yourself to become completely absorbed in it.

Several types of practice are popular for this. These include qigong, tai chi, and yoga. Ideally, look for a class in your area so that you can learn from an expert. If you can't find one, try searching for videos online. There are also text articles and photos online, or you could get a book. Typically, you memorize a set of poses that flow together into a routine. Sun Salutations in yoga are one famous example. Performing the same routine becomes a comforting ritual.

Walking is among the most popular types of moving meditation. If you walk places instead of always driving, then you give yourself time to experience more of the world. First, focus on your breath, then on how your body feels. Use all of your senses. Listen to the birds singing. Feel your feet against the ground. Do you smell flowers, mud, cut grass, fallen leaves, cooking smells, or something else? Taste the water in your bottle or an energy snack. Imagine yourself as a moving part of the living universe. This way, your meditation practice becomes part of your everyday life.

Some people turn crafts into moving meditations. Almost anything can work. Among the most popular are knitting and crochet. For this, you want a simple pattern that you can do without thinking too hard or referring to notes. Now is not the time to learn a compli-cated new stitch. A scarf or potholder works well for a shape because they're simple. Choose a yarn that feels good to touch, preferably a natural fiber like wool or cotton. Focus on your breath and on your hands. Think about how your knitting needles or crochet hook loop the yarn around itself to form fabric. Let yourself get lost in the gen-tle rhythm and just move without overthinking it.

Another category is everyday activities. These are things we often do mindlessly that we could do mindfully instead. Think about brushing your hair, how you use the same smooth stroke over and over again. You could turn that into a moving meditation on self-care. Shucking corn, cooking food, and washing the dishes are other examples. Zen monks have a saying for seeking enlight-enment: "Chop wood, carry water." One infamous example is the doorway exercise, which simply requires you to pause and reflect for a moment before you pass through a door. Actually remem-bering to do this *before* you walk through, rather than after, is a lot harder than it sounds.

Many different activities can serve as moving meditations. Mindfulness is something you can practice wherever you are as you go through your day.

Ostara Ritual

Lupa

OSTARA IS OFTEN SEEN as one of the lighter, more "friendly" sabbats compared to Samhain's themes of harvest and mortality or Yule's longest night. There's nothing wrong with keeping a positive, fertile spin on your festivities, of course. But every time of year has its blessings and challenges, and the turn of spring is no guarantee of an easy time. This ritual is a celebration of the warmer days ahead but also a petition for spiritual aid in surviving the lean times until our efforts come to fruition.

Calling on Community

First, go outside and collect leaves, flowers, and other materials from any plants you find. If possible, find some that are producing fresh, green growth as well as others that are still dry and dormant. For those with a mild spring where local flora area largely alive and thriving, look for some of last year's dead, dry leaves, stems, and other remains. Conversely, if conditions are cold enough that all the plants are still in dormancy and there's not a bit of green to be found, just gather whatever you can find and perhaps supplement with some fresh growth from houseplants.

Next, gather or create representations of some of your local wild animals, focusing not just on more noticeable mammals and birds but also reptiles, amphibians, fish, insects, and other smaller beings. If you have statues or small pictures, you may use them, or make your own with the art supplies of your choice. (You don't have to be a professional-level artist for this.)

Once you have collected these materials, set up your ritual space and open it to the sacred in whatever way you see fit. Arrange the plants in a circle on your altar, with the greener ones on the upper half and the drier specimens on the lower. As you place each plant, call upon the archetypal spirit that protects its species:

Hear me, oh spirit of [plant species], and join me on this equinox [day/night]. Whether your kin still rest within the soil or have burst forth in flower, you are welcome in this celebration of the season.

Next, place each animal's symbol on the circle of plants. Think about what these animals' lives may be like right now. Are they awake and moving around or hibernating? What food sources are available to them, and how difficult are they to access? Do they face predation or competition from other species? What adaptations do they have to help them survive and thrive during this balancing point of the year? Place each animal's symbol on the circle in a place you feel represents how difficult its life may be right now. A species that struggles this time of year may be in the middle of the dried plants, while one that thrives in these conditions can be set on the green ones. As you do so, call upon each species' archetypal spirit:

Hear me, oh spirit of [animal species], and join me on this equinox [day/night]. Whether your kin are still dormant in their winter rest or awake and moving about, you are welcome in this celebration of the season.

Now, consider the interactions between various species and ask the spirits to aid you if need be. Some animals may be competitive, such as two species fighting for the same nesting sites. In North

America, for example, invasive European starlings push bluebirds out of nest boxes and may even kill these native birds in the process. But there is cooperation as well, like ravens leading wolves to potential prey and then joining in the feast once a kill is made. The predator-prey relationship is full of checks and balances, where the abundance or scarcity of one species affects the other similarly. And, of course, prey animals are nowhere near as helpless or gentle as is often assumed, and many predators have been injured or killed by their quarry's defenses, like a lion whose neck is broken by a vicious kick from a zebra.

Lay pieces of yarn or string between pairs of animals. You might use red for competition, blue for collaboration, and black for predation, as one suggestion. If two species have more than one sort of relationship, such as both competition and predation, connect them with both colors. By the time you are done, you should have a complex webwork linking these many animals.

Next, link animals with plants they have relationships with, again asking for spiritual help as needed. An animal that grazes on grass (predation) may be connected with a black cord, while one that relies on a tree or shrub for shelter could be linked via a blue one. You can even lay yarn between plants if you know enough about their interactions. Two species of trees that fight for the same access to sunlight at the top of the canopy could have a red thread between them, for example.

Place your hands on this intricate weaving of yarn or string. Imagine the energy that flows among all these species lighting up the cords, sifting in from the outdoor nature around you and settling into the representation you've created. Consider how your own life, and human societies in general, are similarly complex.

Now, think of the challenges you currently face, whether they are difficult relationships with other people, social disadvantages, health issues, or other problems. For each one, cut a piece of red or black yarn (depending on whether you think competition or predation is a better analogue), or choose another yarn color that you feel fits each one best. As you do so, say to the spirits:

I may not be a wild being in nature, but I face tribulations now just as you do. This cord represents the challenge presented to me by [person/problem] and how I struggle with [briefly explain the impact on your life]. I ask you to help me find the strength, cleverness, and resilience to meet this challenge so I may survive to see better times.

Place your hands over the webwork of cords, and allow those spirits who wish to aid you to send their energy through your weaving. If you feel moved to do so, thank each one as you recognize their presence.

Think of all those with whom you have mutually supportive relationships or various influences in your life that have made it better, such as good health, enjoyable and sustainable employment, etc. For each of these, cut a piece of blue yarn and lay it over the webwork. As you do so, say to the spirits:

Like you, I do not exist in isolation but as part of a complex community. This cord represents my relationship with [person/influence] and how they help me thrive by [briefly explain your connection]. I ask you to help me preserve this precious connection so that I may be able to weather the lean times and be supportive to others in turn.

Again, place your hands over the webwork and feel the energy of the spirits who wish to aid you flowing through the cords. Thank them as they do so if you wish.

Finally, consider the challenges that your local nature may face and think of some way you may be able to help them. You might remove invasive plants and add native ones to return balance to your local ecosystem, or create a clean water source for local animals, even if it is a simple dish that you put out in your yard or garden, sterilizing it every time you refill it. You might also advocate for your local wildlife by contacting elected officials about the negative effects of pesticides and other chemicals, or educating others about how habitat destruction is the leading reason species go extinct. Even if you can only pick one small action to focus on right now, that's enough.

Place your hands on the webwork one more time and send your energy into it to the many beings who are part of this wealth of connections. As you do so, say to the spirits:

I may not be able to fix every problem we face, but I want to offer my service to you in this way: [explain the action you have promised to take]. I thank you for supporting me, and I hope that this will be a fitting way to return your kindness.

Collect the cords and bundle them together; you may also braid or weave them if you prefer. Leave them on or near your altar as a reminder of your connection to your local nature and how you will work together to survive the tough times and make it to better days.

Notes

Notes

Beltane

Celebrating Beltane for Months

Jenny C. Bell

AT SOME POINT ON my Wheel of the Year journey, I came to realize that we don't have to celebrate on the exact day that a sabbat falls, nor do we have to limit our celebration to just one day. I look at the wheel more like a pie with eight slices. Each holiday marks a slice in the year. The pie slice of Beltane in the Northern Hemisphere begins on April 30 and spans until the day before Litha. In this way, you are allowing yourself to step into the vibration of each holiday. And the vibration of Beltane is fertility.

Beltane is on the opposite side of the Wheel of the Year from Samhain, which is a portal of death. Beltane opens the portal to birth. The portals of death and birth are one and the same. Our souls move through the same door on the way out as they do on the way in. Beltane opens this portal and allows you to manifest change. *Manifesting* is pursuing a change that you feel will be good for you. Manifesting is more than wishing or dreaming. It is stating a clear hope and then making the changes you can to make the hope a reality.

Change is our constant. Embracing the change that each holiday brings helps to bring you into harmony. Beltane brings in the energy of fertility. Ostara marks the readiness of the spiritual womb, and Beltane impregnates this womb. Ostara lines up with the astrological new year (Aries season), and now the fullness of spring is evident. This energy is just waiting for you to tune in and harvest it for your own magickal practice. This energy is there for you to work with during the entire time period or vibration of Beltane, not just the day of. Take your time and luxuriate in the entire season of Beltane.

Honoring Fertility

Beltane invites love into your life. This is the time when the fertile maiden goddess is being impregnated by the virile green god. It's a sexy, sensual, and heady time of the year. Dancing, feasting, laughing, playing, and being outdoors are all great ways to celebrate fertility in your own life. Allow yourself to begin to open up like the flowers around you. Bloom.

Taurus and Gemini

According to tropical astrology, the eighth of the year that belongs to the energy of Beltane also falls under the influence of Taurus and Gemini. Taurus season is from April 20 to May 20, and Gemini season goes from May 21 until Litha. Taurus season is a time of enjoying beauty. Venus, the planet of love and money, rules over Taurus, and this time of year often has people seeking comfort and luxury. Taurus's influence invites you to engage in real self-care, whereas Gemini season has you leaving your cocoon to be a social butterfly. Gemini season follows the fertile time of Taurus and invites you to get out and shine. Gemini is ruled by chatty Mercury, and this season has you finally wanting to leave the home and garden and get together with others. Use this spark of sociability to make summer plans and build community.

Allies of Beltane

The following is a list of different allies you can add to your life. You can work with these allies at any time, but the vibration of Beltane is especially compatible.

Plants

Flowers of all kinds bloom at this time. Passionflower is a great herbal ally, as it helps to ease any anxiety you may be feeling with the flow of busyness that seems to pick up during this time. Drinking hibiscus tea will help to flush out toxins and bring you back into balance.

Crystals

Rose quartz especially opens you to love and receiving at this time. Allow love to take root in your energy. Meditate with holed stones, or hagstones, or place them on your altar to symbolize fertility and opening communication with the Fae realm. Emerald, green aventurine, and jade are all great choices to help you open up to the natural healing of fertility during Beltane season.

Deities

Any deity pair that is a strong union like Frigg and Odin or Isis and Osiris are good choices to honor and meditate with. This is also a good time to work with mother goddesses to help you honor the fertility within and around you. You might enjoy working with fertility goddesses such as Venus or Diana. Yes, even those who cannot bear children can be fertile with ideas, gratitude, and creations. Cernunnos is an amazing god to choose to work with at this time. He is a virile horned god who can help you get back to feeling sensual and empowered in your sexuality.

Activities to Tune In To

Beltane is a perfect time to invite in the subtle yet potent energy of flower magick. Flowers are blooming, and they are symbolic of fertility. Allow yourself to play with the energy of flowers.

Creating a Flower Essence

A flower essence is a way to capture the vibrational healing of a flower. This is a meditative process that fosters a connection between you and the flower. To make an essence, you will need a clean jar half full of clean drinking water and an offering for the flower such as incense, a crystal, or a song. Begin by opening sacred space around yourself and centering. Let your intuition lead you to a flower that seems like a healer for you at this time. The flower could be growing in your own yard or in a place where you are allowed to forage. Hold the bloom in your hands and close your eyes, asking if the flower is right for you. If you feel a yes, then gently snip the bloom and let it fall into the jar of water. Then leave your offering.

Next, allow the bloom to sit in the water in the sunshine for about three hours. After three hours, gently remove the flower and fill the rest of the jar with brandy. This jar is now what is referred to as the *mother essence*. Make sure to label the jar with the flower and date, and gently shake it. While shaking, think of what healing you feel the flower will give you. Next, pour some of the mother essence into a smaller dropper bottle, filling this bottle halfway and then adding water to fill the other half. This is now the essence you can use in magick. It can be added to spells, anointed on your body, or you can even add it to your food or drinks.

Flower Grid

A flower grid is what an artist might call a flat lay or a Buddhist might call a mandala. But for witches and Pagans, it's an intentionally created piece of art that serves a spiritual purpose. Grids can be made out of stones, crystals, feathers, bones and, in this case, flowers. When creating a grid, first determine a purpose or intention. It may be to celebrate the fertility in your own life or to honor a certain god or goddess. You may want to connect this grid to the ritual of connecting to your spirit guides at the end of this sabbat's section. Next, decide where you will make this grid. Will it live on your altar for the Beltane season? Will it adorn a part of your yard, or will it be something that you later press and keep forever?

Once you have decided your intention for your grid, purposefully choose flowers. If you are collecting through foraging, make sure to ask each flower, never take endangered flowers, never take more than you need, and never take the first one you see. If you are buying flowers, try to shop at eco-friendly and ethical florists. For the grid, you can use the whole bloom or take the bloom apart to use separate petals.

In general, use your intuition to choose flowers, but here are some common flower meanings to help you:

- Daisy: A youthful and happy flower. Their energy invites fairies.
- Lavender: Brings a sense of calm and peace. It can also represent the crown chakra or spiritual awakening with its deep purple hue. It is also a cleansing flower.
- Lilac: Not only edible with a strong scent but also used for protection.
- Lilies: Deeply feminine and can be used to bring in divine feminine or goddess energy. They are also symbols of peace.
- Rose: Associated with love and romance, but they also have intense thorns, and for this reason can be used in magick to protect.
- Violets: Used for good fortune.

Once you have chosen your flowers based on your intention and intuition, you're ready to create your grid. First, open sacred space and call on whatever deities you would like. State your intention for your grid and ask the flowers to lend their energies. Then create a design that speaks to your desire. You can use a sacred geometry cloth or create your own symbol. You may add herbs, stones, seashells, or other symbolic objects. Make it beautiful, and take your time. When you are done, dedicate your grid to its purpose and close your circle.

Flower Pressing

If you keep a Book of Shadows, a fun activity for Beltane is to take a walk around your yard or in your area collecting one of every kind of flower growing at this time. Make sure to follow an honorable harvest, asking each flower before collecting. Then, once home, gently arrange your blooms on a blank page of your book. Next, carefully close your book and put some heavier books or weights on top to help flatten your blooms. Allow them to sit for at least a week to be pressed and begin to dry. Once they are dry, carefully lift any that are not stuck to the page and apply some glue either to the paper or the back of the flower and leave to dry. If you do this activity every year in the same area, you will see which flowers come and go.

Adorning Your Altar

Taurus season will have you wanting to beautify your home, and you should definitely extend this energy to your Beltane altar. Beltane is such a regenerative and delightful time of year. Adorn your altar with what feels beautiful for you or use some of the following ideas.

Womb Symbols

In the lushness of spring, your altar may want to reflect the bounty of flowers and plants available. Cauldrons, hollow seashells, and bowls represent the feminine because of their womb-like ability to contain. You can fill bowls with flowers, water, crystals, seashells, or anything else that feels fertile.

Flowers

On your altar, bring in fresh flowers, seeds, and potted plants. If you cannot get fresh flowers, try drawing or painting some on rocks, cloth, or pieces of wood to reuse again and again.

Baby Animals

Collect photos or statues of baby animals to represent the fertility of this time. You can find a lot of these decorations, as well as eggs, around Easter and use them on your Ostara and Beltane altars.

Maiden Goddesses or Mother Goddesse

Use oracle cards or statues of maiden or mother goddesses to adorn your altar. Choose maidens if you feel like you need the strong warrior energy or mothers if you need more nurturing.

Green Man or Horned Gods

Statues, oracle cards, or shed antlers can all represent the Horned God. The Green Man is fairly popular, and statues or masks are easy to find to add near or on your altar.

Conclusion

Allow yourself to be a meandering bumblebee this Beltane. Drift happily from flower to flower. Use them to make essences, grids, and artwork. Place them on your altar, put them in your hair, and place them in vases around your home. Generally give in to the sensuality that they invoke. Invite fertility into your life by taking an attitude of gratitude. Be grateful for each and every simple pleasure: the feel of a soft, worn T-shirt, the taste of chocolate, the smile of a friend, etc. Allow ideas to surface and creativity to flow.

Resources

Cunningham, Scott. *Cunningham's Encyclopedia of Magical Herbs.* Llewellyn Publications, 2007.

Holm, Melinda Lee. *Your Magickal Year: Transform Your Life Through the Seasons of the Zodiac.* CICO Books, 2022.

McCoy, Edain. *Sabbats: A Witch's Approach to Living the Old Ways.* Llewellyn Publications, 2001.

Miernowska, Marysia. *The Witch's Herbal Apothecary: Rituals & Recipes for a Year of Earth Magick and Sacred Medicine Making.* Fair Winds Press, 2023.

Telesco, Patricia. *A Floral Grimoire: Plant Charms, Spells, Recipes, and Rituals.* Crossed Crow Books, 2024.

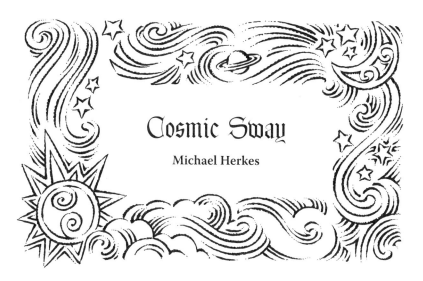

Cosmic Sway

Michael Herkes

As the Wheel of the Year turns, we find ourselves in that magical stretch between Beltane and the summer solstice. This time is ripe with potential, buzzing with the energy of new growth and transformation. It's a season that calls us to embrace both the light and the shadow, to dance with joy and dive deep into our inner worlds.

Observing Beltane and Full Moon in Scorpio

Beltane, that ancient Celtic fire festival, kicks things off on May 1. But this year, we've got an interesting twist. Just as we're lighting our bonfires and dancing around the Maypole, the Full Moon in Scorpio comes creeping in at 1:23 p.m. Talk about a cosmic mashup!

Here we are, celebrating life and fertility, and along comes Scorpio, whispering of mysteries and hidden depths. It's like the universe is giving us a wink and saying, "Hey, remember, true intimacy involves both the light and the dark." This Full Moon is perfect for love magic, but not just the fluffy, hearts-and-flowers kind. We're talking about the deep, soul-stirring stuff. Light some candles, draw a bath infused with rose petals and mugwort, and really connect with what brings you pleasure. Don't be afraid to explore those shadowy corners of your desires.

Pluto Retrograde

Just a few days later, on May 6 at 11:34 a.m., Pluto decides to join the retrograde party. Now, I know some folks get nervous about retrogrades, but Pluto's backward dance is actually a gift. It's like the cosmos is giving us a chance to do some serious soul-searching. Pluto rules transformation, power, and those things we'd rather keep hidden. During this retrograde, which lasts until October 15 at 10:41 p.m., we're being asked to look at where we might be giving our power away or where we're holding on to control too tightly.

It's a great time to journal, to dive into shadow work, to face those parts of ourselves we'd rather ignore. Maybe pull out your tarot deck and have a heart-to-heart with your shadow self. Remember, the goal isn't to banish our darkness but to integrate it to find the wisdom and strength it holds.

Mother's Day and Celebration of the Divine Feminine

As we move into mid-May, we've got Mother's Day on May 10. Now, I know this can be a complicated day for many, but for witches and Pagans, it's a beautiful opportunity to honor the divine feminine in all her forms. Whether you have a relationship with a specific goddess or simply want to celebrate the nurturing, creative force of the universe, take some time to connect.

You might want to create an altar with symbols of motherhood from various cultures. Or take a walk in nature, really tuning in to Mother Earth beneath your feet. If you're feeling crafty, try your hand at making a corn dolly, a traditional symbol of the harvest goddess. Remember, the divine feminine isn't just about biological motherhood—it's about nurturing, creativity, and the power to bring forth life in all its forms.

May and June Moon Magic

The New Moon in Taurus on May 16 at 4:01 p.m. brings us back down to earth. Taurus energy is all about grounding, pleasure, and manifesting in the physical world. This is a perfect time to set intentions around abundance, self-worth, and creating beauty in your life. Maybe plant some seeds—both literal and metaphorical. Taurus loves luxury, so don't be afraid to indulge your senses. Cook a delicious meal, give yourself a massage with luxurious oils, or spend some time in nature really soaking in the beauty around you.

As we round out May, we're treated to a monthly Blue Moon in Sagittarius on May 31 at 4:45 a.m. Now, there's a lot of confusion about what a Blue Moon actually is. Contrary to popular belief, it's not actually blue! It's simply the second Full Moon in a calendar month. But don't let that fool you into thinking it's any less magical.

Sagittarius energy is all about expansion, adventure, and big ideas. Combine that with the magnifying power of a Full Moon and you've got some serious magical potential on your hands. This is a great time for any spells or rituals involving travel, higher education, or expanding your horizons in some way.

You might want to create a vision board for your biggest, wildest dreams. Or perform a ritual to connect with your spirit guides, asking for wisdom and guidance. If you're feeling adventurous, try sleeping under the stars, opening yourself up to prophetic dreams.

As we move into June, we're greeted by a New Moon in Gemini on June 14 at 10:54 p.m. Gemini energy is all about communication, curiosity, and making connections. This is a fantastic time to start a new journal, learn a new form of divination, or connect with like-minded magical folks. Maybe host a small gathering (online or in person) to share knowledge and experiences. Gemini loves variety, so don't be afraid to mix up your magical practice a bit. Try a new technique, work with a different pantheon, or explore a magical tradition you're not familiar with.

Summary

Throughout this whole season, from Beltane to the edge of summer, we're being called to balance opposing energies. We've got the fiery passion of Beltane tempered by Scorpio's watery depths. The grounded practicality of Taurus dances with Sagittarius's expansive dreams. Pluto asks us to dive deep while Gemini encourages us to reach out and connect.

It's a powerful reminder that magic, like life, isn't about choosing one side or the other. It's about finding the balance, dancing between the light and the shadow, embracing both the earth beneath our feet and the stars above.

So as you move through this season, don't be afraid to explore all facets of yourself and your practice. Light your Beltane fires but also honor the darkness. Set practical, earthy goals, but also dream big. Do the deep, transformative work, but also remember to play and explore. May this season bring you growth, transformation, and a deeper connection to your magical path.

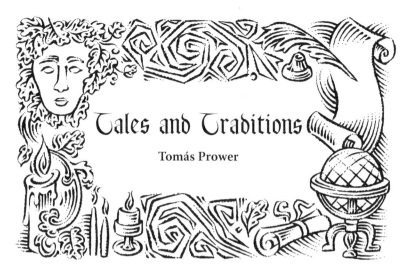

Tales and Traditions

Tomás Prower

BELTANE MARKS THE BEGINNING of the warm season. The lingering and sometimes sporadic coldness in early and mid-spring is finally over, and everyone can look forward to long days of warmth and ripeness. To a greater degree than other sabbats, Beltane is one of the more sexualized. Fertility imagery abounds, most notably in the phallic Maypole and interlocking dance of men and women intertwining their ribbons with each other. Flowers, the reproductive organs of blossoming plants, are given as gifts, and their intoxicating perfume mingles with our own pheromones of desire. It is a time of joy and vibrancy both in carnal pleasure and romantic love. In both endeavors, however, it is love that gets us what we want. Both sex and romance are gained by giving love, and perhaps Beltane's lesson of love as our greatest weapon extends into all endeavors in our life as well.

Kamapua'a: The Seductive Strength of Love

In the mythology of Native Hawaiians, Kamapua'a is a demigod. The sexual union of his divine motther, Hina (goddess of the moon), with a mortal father resulted in a very unique birth that left him as half this and half that in a way similar to his halfness in being both mortal and divine, for his physique was that of both pig and man. To most Westerners who are more familiar with the mythologies and lore of Europe than of Polynesia, a first glance at Kamapua'a would instantly evoke images and recollections of the Greek deity Pan and his half-goat, half-man physique. And though this is an imperfect comparison (as crosscultural comparisons almost always are due to the amount of cultural context that gets lost or muddled in translations just as much as words or languages), there does exist a level of overlap between them. Similar to Pan, Kamapua'a is seen as more "wild" than other divinities and known to revel in the uncomplicated, pastoral, base pleasures of life. Unlike Pan, however, Kamapua'a holds sacred patronage over both sexuality *and* battle.

Not too often in the mighty pantheons of cultures around the world are the dominions of both sex and battle shared by a single divinity. Seemingly at odds, sex gods tend to have a lascivious nature to them, an immodest pride in their own vulgarity, and a lack of self-control that allows them to live a kind of carefree, undisciplined life. They confront life a day at a time with fluid ease. Battle deities trend toward the opposite in that they are highly disciplined, live by the strategic foreplanning needed of battle, and are rarely capricious or ever at ease. Still, as Kamapua'a shows, both are one and the same—opposite sides of the same coin, perhaps. Both sex and battle are hot-blooded endeavors ultimately ruled neither by the mind or emotion but by basic instinct.

When we encounter someone who stirs sexual desire within us and inflames our passions to pursue pleasure, love is the secret weapon that allows us to achieve fulfillment. Through courtship, wooing, and words and actions that show a person they are loved by us, sex is given more readily. Whether one is sincere or not in their declarations of love and romance is another matter, but regardless of sincerity, the best way of winning the game of seduction is through a show of love. Even if this showing is just a "show," the effect is just as powerful.

In battle, too, love is what ultimately conquers. Brute force may win the actual battle, but it doesn't really end the war. Submission of an enemy from overpowering them only results in a temporary peace until the enemy, humiliated and vengefully longing to get back at you, is strong enough to fight again. As ironic and clichéd as it may seem, love is the only thing that truly ends the cycle of violence, for love is what stops making an enemy an enemy, and without an enemy to fight, all battles are truly over. This is as true in the grand theaters of war as it is in the stages of our daily life. Someone may have wronged us in some way, but in our festering for revenge, whether justified or not, we keep the wound open and fresh, as if it has been newly inflicted upon us with every new day. Love, via forgiveness, is what ultimately heals us and ends the indefinitely long effects of things done unto us.

Kamapua'a utilized this weapon of love in one particular battle against the volcanic goddess Pele. According to Hawaiian legends, Kamapua'a and Pele had a turbulent relationship with one another and would get in fights together. One day, the two finally agreed to resolve all their issues via a one-on-one fight. On the eve before this fight, however, Pele came up with a dirty trick to give her an advantage in combat. She convinced two of her brothers to beat up Kamapua'a in the night so that the next day Kamapua'a would already be weak and injured. Upon reaching Kamapua'a, though, Pele's brothers don't receive the violent resistance they were expecting from a deity of battle. Instead, Kamapua'a calls upon Lonoikiaweawealoha (god of love) to help him seduce them. With the powers of love aiding in his own powers of sexuality, a physicality of a different nature took place that night—an erotic orgy that left Kamapua'a's would-be attackers too tired and satisfied to harm him in any way to which he did not consent. Thus, on the next day, Kamapua'a was spry and particularly relaxed and ready to do combat with Pele.

What's particularly interesting about this Hawaiian myth, especially as to how it relates to the lessons of Beltane, is that Kamapua'a enlisted the help of Lonoikiaweawealoha. One would think that the deity of sexuality would be well within his wheelhouse in seducing two enemies into a night of physically exhaustive sex with him, but instead, the deity of sexuality asked for help from the god of love. Thus, sexuality alone doesn't win consent, but rather, love is the key to sex.

So, as the sexuality of the season displays itself, remember that love is what gives sexuality its winning edge. Seduction can go very far, but it doesn't go far enough on its own. Adding a little authentic love into your May Day courtships will help you win the battle, just as it will help us all in winning our own battles.

Beasts and Treats

Nathan M. Hall

NEXT TO SAMHAIN, BELTANE is my second-favorite holiday. The veil once again has grown thin, but this time, the Fae are crossing over for a visit. These recipes are great for a holiday that leaves you feeling light, bouncy, and wanting to dance or enjoy any of the other active pleasures of the season!

Butter-Basted Trout with Lemon and Capers

If you're making the following recipes together for one meal, take care to make the Carrot Ribbon Salad and Farro with Goat Cheese first. The fish will be the last element and cooks very quickly, so it's best to have everything set and ready to go. Serve White Wine Spritzers to your guests and then excuse yourself to cook the trout. You'll be back at the table before they finish their drinks.

Prep time: 1 minutes
Cooking time: 8–10 minutes
Servings: 4

1½ pounds trout fillets, skin on (four 6-ounce fillets)
Pinch of kosher salt
Fresh ground pepper
2 lemons, 1 juiced and 1 sliced

2 tablespoons neutral oil like peanut or grapeseed

3 tablespoons salted Irish butter (regular butter in a pinch)

3 tablespoons capers, drained

Prepare 4 approximately 6-ounce trout fillets on a small baking sheet or platter. Don't worry about scaling, just pat dry with a paper towel and sprinkle with kosher salt, ground pepper, and a squeeze of lemon.

Heat a pan on medium-high heat, drizzling oil into the pan when it's hot and nearly smoking. Place the fish, skin-side down, into the pan. Let sear undisturbed for 4–5 minutes until the fillets have a nice golden color underneath. Carefully (using two spatulas if necessary) flip each of the fillets over. Lower the temp to medium and drop in butter in pieces around the fillets and let melt and begin to sizzle. Tilt the pan at a 30-degree angle to encourage the butter and juices to pool at the bottom. With a spoon, begin scooping up and splashing the hot butter over the fillets, then set back on heat for a minute. Continue alternating between basting and letting sit on heat until fish is completely cooked through.

Transfer to plates and put capers in the pan. Roll the capers around, using a circular motion with the pan to heat through, and then spoon butter and capers over the top of each fillet before bringing to the table.

Carrot Ribbon Salad

As simple as it is elegant, the great thing about this recipe is that a little goes a long way, but if you're worried that two carrots won't be enough, just have some extras on hand.

Prep time: 8 minutes

Servings: 4

1 clove garlic

4 tablespoons olive oil

2 tablespoons apple cider vinegar

1 teaspoon sea salt, or more to taste

Fresh ground pepper
2 large carrots

Start by making the dressing, mincing one clove of garlic (or use a garlic press) and placing into a bowl followed by the olive oil, apple cider vinegar, salt, and pepper. Whisk well and let sit while you prep the carrots.

For the carrots, peel the outer layer of skin off and compost. Begin peeling long, thin ribbons from the top to the bottom. It will be monotonous and feel like it's taking longer than it should. I recommend using what are often referred to as *Y-peelers*, so-called because the handle and blade holder elements form a Y shape. They seem to hold up to cutting long ribbons better than the standard kitchen peelers.

Once you've got a nice pile of ribbons, give the dressing a taste and adjust with more salt as needed. (Remember, if your lips pucker from the vinegar, add more salt!) Mix the carrots with the dressing and, using a pair of forks, lift out a serving and pile onto individual plates for serving. They should make a nice, high pile on the plate that roughly resembles a bird's nest.

Farro with Goat Cheese

Farro is one of the grains that was originally cultivated in the Fertile Crescent and has been nourishing humanity with its high-fiber and high-protein kernels ever since. It has a reputation for taking a long time to make, but pearled farro removes the harder bran layer and speeds up the process.

Prep time: 15 minutes
Cooking time: 15–20 minutes
Servings: 4–6

3 cups chicken or vegetable broth
1 tablespoon olive oil
1 cup pearled farro (makes 4 servings, increase by ½ cup for 6)
1 tablespoon Beltane seasoning blend (more if desired)

2 parts oregano

1 part crushed rosemary

1 part thyme

1 part fennel

1 part garlic granules

½ red onion, sliced and cooked through in a pan

4 ounces goat cheese (Keep in refrigerator until ready to use.)

1 pint grape tomatoes, cut in half

1 bunch parsley, chopped

This dish will be served at room temperature, so have a sheet pan handy to let the farro cool after it has cooked.

Add broth to a pot with a tablespoon of olive oil, cover, and bring to a boil. Add in the farro, bring back up to a boil, and then reduce heat to low and keep simmering for 15–20 minutes. Farro is ready when it has an al dente quality and is slightly springy to chew. Don't overcook, as it will turn mushy like oatmeal. When finished, drain off any excess liquid and spread out over the sheet pan to cool. Sprinkle the Beltane seasoning and red onions over the top.

In the meantime, grab the goat cheese from the refrigerator and cut in half lengthwise and then cut those halves lengthwise again. Follow up by cutting across the lengths, making small, thumbnail-sized chunks of cheese. Goat cheese can get messy the warmer it gets, so be prompt while cutting.

Scrape all of the farro off of the sheet tray into a serving bowl and stir in the tomatoes and goat cheese. Top with the chopped parsley and incorporate roughly with two or three stirs and serve.

White Wine Spritzer

Tasty, light, and refreshing, this drink is perfect as an aperitif or served alongside the fish at the table.

Prep time: 2 minutes

Servings: 1

Ice
¾ cup chilled white wine (I like a dry wine like sauvignon blanc)
¼ cup club soda
Lemon rind

Add as much ice as you prefer to a stemmed glass, fill about three quarters with white wine, and top with club soda. Garnish with a lemon rind you peeled from the lemons used in the trout recipe and sip to your heart's content.

Crafty Crafts

Raechel Henderson

BELTANE SEES THE WORLD flush with growth. Birds, bees, and all other manner of life are in abundance. Fruit is ripening and flowers are in full bloom. One of the old Celtic fire festivals, Beltane is often considered the "sexy" sabbat with its Maypoles and talk of the goddess and god consummating their union. This fecund abundance urges us to get out of the house and into nature to enjoy the height of spring and the coming of summer. To that end, it is the perfect time to collect herbs and wildflowers to create beautiful and useful smoke cleansing bundles.

Herb Smoke Cleansing Bundles

Smoke cleansing is seen throughout history and the modern-day world. Cedar, rosemary, pine, mugwort, and lavender are all herbs that have been traditionally used in various paths for their cleansing properties and pleasant scents. In Scottish practice, the activity is called *saining* and involves burning juniper to use the smoke to cleanse a space.

Note that white sage and palo santo are not mentioned. The first is used by Indigenous peoples in their smudge ceremonies and considered a closed practice. The second, like white sage, is in danger of being overharvested. It is better to take some time and do research into your ancestors and cultural history to see what they used rather than grabbing that bundle of white sage being sold for $14.99 at your local metaphysical store.

The benefit of smoke cleansing is twofold: On a practical level, it helps to freshen the air, which can often help immensely when you feel like there are stale or unwanted odors in your space. Magically, however, smoke cleansing breaks up that stagnant energy so that you can bring in other, more beneficial energies to your home.

Most of the herbs mentioned above can be bought from your local supermarket, while others like juniper and pine can be foraged. When foraging, make sure that you are only taking what you need and from places that you are allowed to forage in. If you can, look for juniper or pine growing away from roadsides, as they will have absorbed the fumes from passing traffic. Consider leaving an offering (such as the Non-Salt Dough Offering Coins on page 151) when you take the juniper.

If you forage your herbs, make sure to let them sit for a few minutes before you start working with them. This allows for any insects that might have hitched a ride in with the plants to make their exit. It isn't suggested to wash the herbs before you start bundling them, as excess moisture could lead to the growth of mold when they're drying.

Materials
Slips of paper
Fresh herbs like rosemary, lavender, juniper, and pine
Twine, cotton, or hemp cording

Tools
Pencil or pen
Scissors

Cost: $0–$20. The main cost will be the herbs, depending on where you buy them or whether you forage them.

Time spent: 10 minutes to make the bundles, and 1–2 weeks for them to dry

Instructions

Create sacred space to work in according to your path. Start by writing down information on slips of paper about the herbs you are using so you can label your bundles. Include information such as the common and scientific names of the herbs, what their correspondences are, the date they were gathered, and when the bundle was made.

Assemble your bundle of herbs. You want them to be between 4–5 inches in diameter and about 6 inches long. Use scissors to cut the herbs down to the right length if necessary.

Cut a piece of twine, cotton, or hemp cording about 30 inches long. Tie a loop at one end of the twine. Starting at the bottom of the bundle, wrap the loop end of the twine around the bundle, threading the other end of the twine through the loop and pulling it tightly around the bundle to secure it.

Wrap the twine around the herb bundle from the bottom to the top. Once you've reached the top, wrap the twine again down the herb bundle to the bottom where you started. Wrap the twine tightly around the herbs, as they will shrink slightly while the bundle dries. As you are working, think about the herbs that you are bundling together. What does it mean to cleanse a space? Where does that energy go when you smoke cleanse? Do you envision it being pushed out of the way or leaving through an open door or window, perhaps? Or do you see it as being broken up by the smoke until it dissipates, leaving behind nothing but the purifying energies of the smoke bundle? Thinking about this now and working on your visualization technique will help when you use the bundle to actually cleanse a space. It helps build your visualization muscles long before you need to put them into practice.

When you reach the bottom of the herb bundle, wrap the twine around it several times and then tie it off. Cut off the excess twine.

Hang your bundles in a place where they are out of direct sunlight and there is air flow around them. Let them hang for 1–2 weeks so they can dry thoroughly. Attach your labels to each herb bundle so that you know what they are, as herbs can often look very similar once they have dried.

When your bundles are dry, store them in a cool, dry place. Once dry, and if properly stored, they should last you a year or longer. However, as time goes by, the volatile oils in the herbs will start to break down and the bundles won't be as effective, so use them often and liberally. You can always make more.

To use them, simply light the top end of the bundle and then blow out the flames. Waft the smoke into the areas that you wish to cleanse. If you are cleansing spaces like your home, make sure the smoke goes into corners, cupboards, closets, and drawers for the most effective cleansing.

Also ensure that there is at least one open window or door for the energy that is being cleansed to escape out of. Otherwise, you'll just be moving that energy from room to room. After you have cleansed your space, you may want to lay down a foundation of energy that is more active and beneficial to you and your home.

Beltane Meditations

Elizabeth Barrette

AT BELTANE, SPRING IS in full swing. Outdoors, everything is blooming and the world is full of young animals learning to live. This sabbat is about passion and creation. The body and spirit are surging with life. Now is a good time for meditations that focus on the self. The more you know about yourself, the better equipped you are to face any of life's challenges calmly and effectively.

Body Scan Meditations

There are various body scan meditations designed to raise awareness of your physical self and your emotions as they manifest in bodily sensations. They help with mindfulness and with grounding you in the here and now. They also establish the difference between "you" and "not-you," which some people find challenging to distinguish. They are a vital foundation for self-work and healthy boundaries. They can relieve pain, depression and anxiety, tension, and self-loathing. They also tend to improve the quality of your sleep at night. If you experience difficulties with your body or accepting it the way it is, then these are one of the best ways to deal with that.

Most people prefer to do this meditation while lying in bed, face up. However, you can do it anywhere, especially if you feel the need for grounding and self-awareness during your day. It works sitting in a chair or standing. Being still is better than moving so that you can focus on what you're feeling instead of what you're doing.

Think about how you divide your body. For this meditation, you will be paying attention to one part at a time, so decide what parts you want to define. You might prefer larger, simpler divisions or smaller, more precise ones. Consider feet (toes, arches, ankles), legs (calves, knees, thighs), hips (buttocks, genitals), torso (belly, chest, back), hands (fingers, palms, wrists), arms (forearms, elbows, upper arms, shoulders), head (neck, face). Body scans typically move from feet to head. In order to help with focusing on specific body parts, people often use a technique called *progressive muscle relaxation* where you tense and relax each muscle group in turn; this is optional and not required for the body scan itself.

This is one type of meditation where you *don't* set aside thoughts and sensations as they come up. The whole point is to notice everything you experience while focusing on one particular body part. Those "random" thoughts may be connected to your body in some way, like if focusing on your shoulders makes you think of your whole to-do list, then maybe you feel that those things are weighing you down. A body scan makes you aware of these things. You may or may not choose to do anything about them later; that's not important now. Just loop back to where you were and continue to the next body part.

First, lie down or sit in a comfortable position. Take a few deep breaths and focus on your breathing. Make it slow and deep as you begin to relax. Feel the temperature of the room, the surface you rest on, perhaps clothes or sheets against your skin.

Concentrate on your toes. Allow yourself to feel whatever is present. Then move your awareness up your body, focusing on one part at a time. Observe how the sensations in your body flux and change and how your feelings about them shift also. Accept your body as it is in this moment without judgment. All things change with time, and the body, too, is impermanent, just a vessel that you inhabit for a time before passing on. Be aware of it but not limited by it.

Self-Inquiry Meditation

Much of mindfulness is about self-awareness. This goes beyond calm and relaxation to touch the core of who you are. In order to find inner peace and live in the moment, you must understand who you are and why you are here. This typically requires spending time in solitude and introspection. You are worth that time. If you don't feel like it yet, then sit with that idea and yourself for a while. You will get the hang of it.

Self-inquiry is a bit more advanced than some of the other meditations. It requires that you already know how to get your mind quiet enough to take a good look at yourself without thoughts bounding about like excited monkeys. You need the ability to distinguish between the permanent and the impermanent, which enables you to tell what is actually part of your true nature and what is just a stage. You also have to be honest about what you want from this. It's not necessarily easy, so you may need to work your way up to it. That's okay. These things take practice.

Begin in your favorite meditative pose. Take a few deep breaths. Draw your attention to your breath. Quiet your mind. Once you are calm, begin to examine your existence. Who are you? What makes you who you are? How would someone recognize you if you suddenly had a different body? Why are you here? Are you fulfilling your life purpose? What are we? What is life? What is all this here for?

Think deeper. You are aware of your body and aware of your spirit. You know that you are—but how do you know it? Where is that feeling of "I" coming from? Search for it the way you would search for a physical feeling, like if you were too hot, you might realize it's the side of you facing the sun, but this is inside your mind. The more you do this, the more everyday layers fall away until you can reach the core of yourself. Sit with that core and observe your true nature. Let that guide you through your life.

With self-inquiry meditation, you go through a cycle of asking yourself questions and trying out different answers. Figure out what you are, what you want, what you are here to do. Test that with imagination, visualizing yourself enjoying that future in as much detail as possible. Take action with a few steps in that direction, then ask how you feel about your progress. Do these things feel like "you" to you? Why or why not? Ideally, you should discover things that make you feel more like yourself. Record how you feel as precisely as possible. You can use words, collage, drawing, music, dance, or whatever other media feels right to you. It doesn't have to be great art; it just needs to express your feelings. This will help you find your way, wherever you are going.

Meditation comes in many forms and brings plenty of benefits. You can explore different styles until you find some that you like.

Beltane Ritual

Jenny C. Bell

BELTANE IS A TIME you can harness the thinning of veils to connect deeper with the invisible world. Many of us use the energy of Samhain to connect with our ancestors and heal past trauma. Samhain is a reflective, waning time, whereas Beltane is a projective, waxing time. Since the energy of Beltane is life and not death, this makes it a perfect opportunity to connect with your spirit guides to manifest positive changes in your life. This is a time to move forward and call on those around you to help you move in the direction you desire. You can perform this ritual anytime during the energy of Beltane.

Everyone has a group of guides that are with them in this life and in some cases have been with them for several lives. Your guides are a team that is unique to you. Like deities and angels, spirit guides tend to not help unless asked. It's an illusion that you go through this life alone. From the moment you are born, there are invisible helpers and other beings around you. Your guides are the ones that send you signs, give you insight, and if asked, offer protection.

Connecting with Spirit Guides for Manifestation

In this ritual, you will first be guided to connect with your spirit guides through meditation. Then you will be guided through a manifesting spell. Next, you will be provided with a divination card spread. And lastly, you will be given time to reflect and journal. You may want to break this ritual over different days or perform all the components in one day, one after another. If you choose to perform this ritual in one go, set aside at least two hours of uninterrupted time to do so. The following is a list of what you will need for this ritual.

Ritual Preparation

Record the meditation on your phone or plan to have a friend read it aloud to you so that you may truly dive into the visualization.

Cleanse and clear yourself, space, and altar. You can use sacred smoke, a selenite wand, the ringing of bells, or any other method that feels like the right type of cleansing for you.

Have a journal and your favorite card deck nearby.

Prepare a green or white novena candle for manifesting. If you can't find a novena candle, any size candle will do. Green represents the goddess and growth. White is an all-purpose color that can be used for any work of magick. If another color feels more appropriate for what you are manifesting, then trust your intuition. Cleanse the candle and anoint it with oils and herbs you associate with manifesting. A great oil to use for any kind of anointing is olive oil. You can choose herbs that you associate with what you're manifesting, but some general manifesting herbs are basil, cinnamon, lavender, and dried orange peel. You may also want to inscribe runes or a sigil for fertility. You can also decorate the outside glass of your candle with symbols, ribbon (like a Maypole) or flowers. You can include any of the allies listed in the introduction article to your altar or candle as well.

Connect with Your Guides

Before you begin this meditation, cast a circle and open sacred space. Allow yourself to be in a position that feels good for your body. Close your eyes and take a series of deep, slow breaths, allowing the body and mind to relax. Visualize or sense your body becoming heavy but your spirit becoming light. See or sense a green light ascend from the earth below you and go to your heart space. Allow this light to enter your heart space. This is the healing energy of the earth. The energy begins to spread from your heart center out through your body. Then it spreads beyond your physical body and surrounds your aura. You are encased in this healing green energy. This energy is raising your vibration and allowing you to regenerate. As the green energy surrounds you, it pulls out anything heavy or unwelcome. This unwanted energy evaporates like smoke. Allow yourself to rest a moment in this healthy and balanced state.

When you are ready, you will call in your spirit guides that want to work with you at this time. You have a large team, and we are only calling in the ones that will help you the most at the present. Take a deep breath, and in your mind or aloud, say the following prayer: "I call on my spirit guides. I appreciate all of you who have been with me, guiding and guarding me. But at this time, I only invite those of my guides who have my best interest in mind and are of the highest vibration to come forward. I am ready to begin anew and blossom and bloom like the earth around me. I invite my spirit guides of highest consciousness to help me manifest a change for the better. I invite you into my circle and into my consciousness now. Reveal yourselves; I am open and ready to listen." You may want to repeat this prayer three times, each time allowing yourself to open more and more.

Now, allow your guides to reveal themselves to you. You may want to visualize a sitting area in your mind where each one comes to join you in a circle or around a flame. Be open, as guides can take many forms and not all are human. Give yourself time to meet each guide, memorizing their faces, and ask for names or what to call them. Some may have messages for you or symbols. When you are done communing with them, say, "Thank you to my spirit guides of highest consciousness for joining me and connecting with me here. I welcome you to stay in this circle as I leave this meditation."

Allow yourself to slowly come out of the meditation. First allow the guides to depart if you are doing this on a separate day from the spell, then allow the green light surrounding you to either remain or dissolve. Come back into your body and the present moment. Record what you saw and anything you have learned. If you don't meet guides in this meditation, pay attention to your dreams and try again in a few days. Sometimes when we first open communication, our guides can be reluctant if they think that we are not ready or not open to what they may look like. Keep reassuring them in daily prayer that you are open to receive them.

Note: If you are not a visual person, then feel free to journal during or after the meditation and see if you can connect better that way.

Beltane Manifesting Spell

If you are conducting this spell on a separate day from the meditation, then first take some time to cast a circle, open sacred space, and center yourself. Next, think about what you are manifesting at this time. This might be a manifestation that you already planted at Ostara or a new one. Get clear on exactly what you want and why. Manifesting works best when we allow ourselves to dream but also get clear on the mundane changes and steps we need to take to get there. When you manifest with the help of your spirit guides, you are opening yourself up to their help and guidance. This might mean that what you originally thought you wanted will shift into something that's actually better for you. This spell opens you up to trusting that your guides have your best interest at the forefront, because they do.

In this spell, you will use the prepared candle, but you can also add some flower essence and create a flower grid as well. When you are ready, sit or stand facing your candle. Take a deep breath, close your eyes, and call on the spirit guides you met in the meditation. "I call into this circle my highest consciousness spirit guides. As the wheel turns once again to fertile Beltane, I manifest with you because I trust that you will open my path before me. As the veils thin, past, present, and future blur, making my dreams a reality. I light this candle and will continue to light it and let it burn, allowing my desires to reach you." Now light the candle and speak clearly what you are manifesting. You may then do whatever other works of magick you have in mind, and when you are ready, close the circle.

How long you allow your candle to burn for is up to you. You may snuff it out each day and repeat the prayer and your manifestations daily, or you might let it burn continuously. (Remember to always burn your candles responsibly and never leave them unattended to prevent fires.) Everyone has their own style; do what feels best for you.

Beltane Flower Spread

You can use this spread with tarot or oracle cards.

1. What is something to be grateful for at this time?
2. What is something to bring into your energy at this time?
3. What is one step you can take toward manifesting your desires?
4. What is a block that needs to be removed to better manifest?
5. What do your guides want you to know at this time?

Journal Reflection

- What have you discovered doing this ritual?
- What are the mundane steps you can take to manifest?
- How will you call on and work with your guides in the future?

Conclusion

Working with your spirit guides is a lifelong journey. As you continue to work with them and invite them into your life, you will learn more about them. You will see guides come and go. Sometimes a guide will seem to take the lead and work with you for months only to then step back later. This kind of change often happens because you have learned a lesson or reached a different part of your spiritual path. Remember, your spirit guide team wants to help you but operates on the premise of free will. They can only help you if you ask. Ask as much as you want and as often as you need.

Notes

Notes

Litha

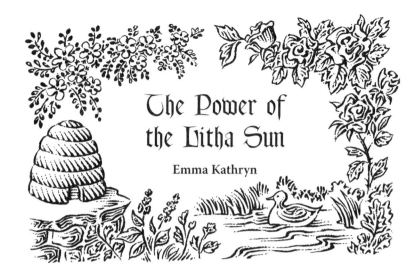

The Power of the Litha Sun

Emma Kathryn

I WAKE EARLY, AS I often do, and slip downstairs, pulling on a jumper to ward off those early morning shivers while the body gets used to the removal of warm covers and cosy sheets. Everyone else in the house sleeps soundly still, except for the dog, and even he only cocks one ear in my general direction, opening one eye just a crack before drifting back into whatever dreams dogs dream.

Coffee made and in hand, I slip into the garden. This is my time, and even more so today, for this is Litha, Midsummer, the longest day and shortest night. And though I try to spend some time every day out of doors, even if it is just to sit for a quiet moment in the dawning clarity and beauty of a new day, it feels a little more special today.

The garden at Litha is a sight to behold indeed. I'm lucky and feel more a steward of this land and space than owner. I moved into a house with a mature and well-maintained garden some twenty odd years ago, with mature trees and shrubs, perfect for my witch heart. And through the lens of my garden, I have come to recognise the markers of each season and the changes that come with them. That's how we all connect with the land and the spirits that reside there—through our observations of the spaces we call home, no matter where they are. But this isn't a static thing though; our inter-actions with those places and the other beings we share them with deepen that connection. It is in this space where I have truly con-nected with nature spirits, and such a connection has added a depth to my witchcraft practice. It's also allowed me to make the Wheel of the Year a personal journey through the year, rediscovering the magic in the land and in the cycles of nature where I live.

The sun is just rising in a clear sky that will darken to cornflower blue in the afternoon, but for now, it is a pale shade, like faded denim. I notice I am not the only one up and out as the blackbird flies into the boughs of the cherry and calls out his melodic song, the perfect soundtrack for this, the longest day. I pass under the tree, letting my hands trail across the rough bark, moving toward the far corner where a linden tree stands sentinel, its flowers per-fuming the cool morning air with their divine scent. I stand for a moment, enjoying the dance of shadow and light as golden sunlight filters through the canopy, before moving on, past the ivy, already alive with the chatter of sparrows. I stand in the centre of the gar-den, eyes open, soaking in the energies of this new day, relishing the assault on my senses of this: Litha in my garden.

There's something special about this place, about this time, and in this moment, it feels as though the day will stretch on in perfect eternity, each moment to be enjoyed and savoured. I always feel as though I have stepped into the pages of *The Secret Garden*, one of my favourite novels and films—a story of camaraderie, hope, enjoyment, and realisation. All of these themes can be found within the Sun tarot card too. In fact, when it comes to Litha, I can't help but think of the Sun. It contains within it the truths of the sabbat and carries lessons for us to learn and enact to ready us for what is to come.

The Sun in the Tarot

The tarot, for those who are unfamiliar with it, is split into two parts: the minor arcana and the major arcana. The minor arcana includes the four suits: pentacles, cups, swords, and wands, and, generally speaking, can be said to represent the day-to-day matters of our lives, such as money, work, relationships, and so on. The major arcana, on the other hand, can be thought of as representing the major themes of life and the archetypes of our journey through it. The Sun card belongs to the major arcana and is the nineteenth card out of twenty two. I often tell my clients that if you were to lay out all the cards in the major arcana, they tell the story of a journey, the lessons of life to be learned and how those lessons shape us as individuals.

So what does the Sun card mean? Well, before we get to that, I have a small exercise I often give to my tarot students to help build understanding. If you have a tarot deck, find the Sun card. If you don't, then find an image of one online. You'll also need a scrap of paper and something to scribble on it with. Now take your card or sit before the image and just look at it, only for a minute or two. What can you see? Are there figures or creatures in the card, and if so, what are they doing? What other imagery is included? What colours do you notice? How do these make you feel? After a minute or so, make notes on what you have seen and how these made you feel. Do you have a general feeling about the card? How do you interpret the imagery and colours? Finally, find the meaning of the card, either online or in the booklet that accompanied your cards, and read what it says about the Sun card. If I were a betting woman, I might be inclined to wager that your scribbled notes are not too dissimilar in meaning to what was written in the booklet. And even if there are some wide differences, everyone's relationship to the cards is unique. What this exercise shows is that the cards speak to us as individuals on a variety of different levels but also hold universal meaning. This is clearest, perhaps, in the Sun card.

This exercise can also be done with Litha where you live. Look out of your window or venture outside and just stand for a minute. Take note of all you see, hear, smell, and feel. This is just one way of connecting the sabbat to the land where you live, no matter where that is.

So, back to meaning: The Sun is generally a positive card, and to think about this, consider what benefits we as a species get from the sun. It is life giving and life promoting. It gives us light to see and warmth. It allows plants and trees to grow, providing food and shelter, and for many people, makes them feel good. It's a joyful time, and if school isn't already out, then it will be soon. If we relate this back to Midsummer, then it becomes easy to see the correlations between Litha and the Sun. If we take the Wheel of the Year as a marker of agricultural activities, then Litha is a bit of an in-between time. The hard work of ploughing and sowing of spring has passed, and the hard work of the harvests at Lughnasadh seems far off. Everything is growing, from the crops in the fields to the animals born in the spring. In the garden, careful parent birds keep watch over fledgling chicks, and the lambs in the field are no longer tiny vulnerable creatures sticking close to their mothers. And because there isn't so much hard work to do, then let the fun times commence!

There is indeed an air of fun at Midsummer paired with a delicious desire to sit, lounge, frolic, and generally enjoy the good times to our heart's content. Of course, our modern way of living means that although we feel like doing all of this, we often can't. But still, this is the time of summer holidays and vacations, of time spent outside simply for the joy it brings. At Litha, it feels easier to indulge our own wants and desires. It's also a great time to work on our own ambitions and dreams, what with all of this potent solar energy that abounds at this time.

But as with any tarot card, the Sun isn't all fun and games and carries with it lessons that must be learned and warnings to be heeded. I often think this is the ultimate everything-in-moderation card. Yes, everything is growing, and this is a potent time to make plans and put in the effort toward your own dreams—that is, if you don't get too caught up in the fun times to be had.

The Sun also reminds us that we can see most clearly in the midday sun, where there are fewer shadows. Sometimes that clarity is stark, and it might be easier to bury your head in the fun times or your own work, but this leads to loss of perspective. While the Moon card asks us to believe in our dreams, the Sun card tempers this with being able to see clearly—the pitfalls and dangers as well as the rewards. The same is true of Litha. This sabbat is the perfect time to stand back and take stock of what has been and what is still to come, to use the solar energy of the longest day to see our victories and our losses with clarity so that we can learn from them. In doing so, we can relish in the magic of the longest day and, of course, the shortest night, for there is indeed a special magic to be found at this time.

One of my favourite plays is Shakespeare's *A Midsummer Night's Dream*, and the themes of it seem to marry quite nicely to everything we have explored thus far: the importance of clarity, to face the reality of our situations, and, of course, fun! It also reminds us that the magic of the sun on the longest day is enhanced by the darkness of the shortest night. I love sitting outside on a midsummer's night with citronella candles lit, solar lights burning gently, and maybe a small fire in the pit. Whether alone or with friends, it is a magical time when the magic of the day mellows. This is a different type of rest than sleep gives; it's a kind of balm for the soul! It's here in the night of Litha that we can explore the lessons of the day, not with the logical mind, but with the magical one.

And so I finish the day where I started—in my garden as the sun is setting on Litha, the longest day. The birds are quiet now, but the pipistrelle bats are just coming out from their roosts beneath the eaves. Their fast movements catch the corner of my eye, backlit against the sky as the reds and oranges give way to darkening purples as the light fades. The shortest night is gently falling. I stand for a moment in the centre, relishing the delicious feel of a most liminal moment and the magic in the air.

However you celebrate Litha and the Midsummer season, may it be filled with clarity, laughter, dreams, and magic!

Cosmic Sway

Michael Herkes

As the Wheel of the Year turns, we find ourselves in that magical stretch between Midsummer and Lammas. It's a time when the Sun's power is at its peak and the earth is bursting with life and abundance. This year, we've got a cosmically chaotic mashup that's sure to keep things interesting.

Observing Midsummer, Cancer Season, and Father's Day

Midsummer, or the summer solstice, falls on June 21, and it's bringing some friends to the party. Not only is it the longest day of the year, but it's also the start of Cancer season and Father's Day. Talk about a power-packed day!

The summer solstice has long been celebrated by our ancestors as a time of light, growth, and abundance. It's when the veil between worlds is thin and magic is particularly potent. Many of us will be lighting bonfires, staying up to greet the dawn, or gathering herbs that are said to be at their most powerful on this day.

Now, throw Cancer energy into the mix, and things get really interesting. Cancer, ruled by the Moon, brings a nurturing, intuitive energy to balance out all that solar power. It's like the universe is reminding us that even in times of outward action and growth, we need to tend to our inner worlds too.

And then there's Father's Day. While not traditionally a Pagan holiday, it does tie in nicely with themes of the divine masculine that many of us work with. This is a great time to honor the nurturing, protective aspects of masculinity, whether that's in our own lives or in our spiritual practice.

This is a simple sunbathing meditation to assist with manifesting your desires for Midsummer. Look for a natural setting where you will be exposed to the Sun's rays. If you have an indoor space with lots of natural light, you can access the Sun from there. Otherwise, go outside to a quiet area where you won't be bothered. On a cushion, mat, or other comfy surface, sit, lay back, or stretch out into a comfortable position.

Close your eyes and imagine the Sun shining down on you. Visualize the Sun's flashing flames as you do this. Now, shift gears and think intensely about whatever it is you wish to manifest. Know that in this moment, the Sun's magic is not only providing your physical body with nourishment, but it is also stimulating the desires in your mind's eye.

Visualize yourself obtaining that wish you desire. After you've finished, give a respectful bow to the Sun, and express your gratitude for the energy it has provided.

Full Moon and Mercury Retrograde

But hold on to your broomsticks, folks, because the cosmic dance is just getting started. On June 29, we've got a Full Moon in Capricorn, and Mercury decides to go retrograde in Cancer on the same day. Talk about mixed signals!

The Capricorn Full Moon is all about structure, discipline, and manifestation. It's a great time to look at your goals and see how far you've come since the last New Moon. But with Mercury going retrograde in emotional Cancer, communication might get a bit…squishy.

Here's a tip: use that Capricorn energy to create some solid structures in your life. Maybe set up a new organization system, or create a ritual space that feels grounding and secure. That way, when Mercury starts throwing emotional curveballs, you've got a stable base to work from.

New Moon in Cancer

As we move into July, we're greeted by a New Moon in Cancer on July 14 at 5:44 a.m. This is a powerful time for setting intentions around home, family, and emotional well-being. Maybe do a ritual bath or create a vision board for your ideal home life. Cancer energy is all about nurturing, so don't forget to include some self-care in your plans.

Saturn Retrograde

Now, brace yourself for July 26 at 3:56 p.m., because Saturn is going retrograde in Aries, and it's sticking around until December 10 at 6:31 p.m. This is…interesting energy, to say the least. Saturn is all about boundaries, structure, and responsibility. Aries, on the other hand, is the cosmic toddler—all enthusiasm and "Let's do it now!"

With Saturn retrograde in Aries, we might find ourselves feeling restricted or held back from charging ahead with our plans. It's like trying to run a marathon with your shoelaces tied together. The key here is patience (not Aries's strong suit) and learning to work within limitations (which Aries hates).

This transit might bring up issues around authority, responsibility, and how we assert ourselves. Keep an eye out for conflicts between your desire for freedom and the need for structure. It's a great time to look at where you might be self-sabotaging by rebelling against necessary boundaries.

Full Moon in Aquarius

We round out July with a Full Moon in Aquarius on July 29 at 10:36 a.m. Aquarius energy is all about innovation, community, and thinking outside the box. This is a great Moon for group rituals or working magic for social causes. It's also a good time to look at where you might be stuck in old patterns and need a fresh perspective.

Summary

Throughout this whole period, from Midsummer to Lammas, we're being asked to balance opposing energies. The fiery, active energy of summer and Aries is being tempered by the watery, emotional vibes of Cancer. The need for structure and boundaries (Saturn and Capricorn) is dancing with the desire for freedom and new ideas (Aries and Aquarius).

It's a powerful reminder that magic, like life, isn't about choosing one side or the other. It's about finding the balance, dancing between the light and the shadow, embracing both the earth beneath our feet and the stars above.

So as you move through this season, don't be afraid to explore all facets of yourself and your practice. Light your Midsummer fires, but also honor the nurturing darkness of Cancer. Set practical, earthy goals with Capricorn, but also dream big with Aquarius. Do the deep, emotional work that Cancer calls for, but also embrace the fiery passion of Aries. May this season bring you growth, transformation, and a deeper connection to your magical path.

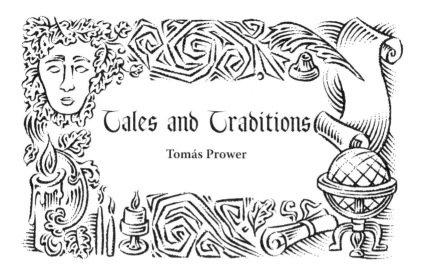

Tales and Traditions

Tomás Prower

LITHA IS THE TIME of the summer solstice, the longest day of the year, and the official beginning of summertime. This is the time of life in its prime. The days are warm, there is plenty of daylight to be able to go out into the world and enjoy it, and our youthful memories of summer vacation all mix into a unique season of the year in which vitality and optimism are dominant. After all, there is a reason why so many religions have their afterlife paradises as places of eternal summer. From Eden to Elysium to even the Theosophists' Summerland and beyond, we humans tend to equate this time of verdant splendor with what we imagine (or hope) awaits us in the next life for ever and ever.

However, Litha is also a turning point in the year. From here on out for the rest of the year, the days will become shorter, and the cold and darkness will come creeping slowly back to strength. And thus, an obvious yet often-overlooked lesson of Litha is to enjoy life in all its primes without clinging to them as eternal, ever aware of the ephemerality of each moment in time.

Guan Yu: Blinding Brightness

In the ancient folktales of China, there exists a legendary figure who exemplifies all the virtues of Litha just as much as he serves as a cautionary tale about the delusion of those same virtues being everlasting. His name is Guan Yu, and though an actual person who lived in China around the mid-third century CE, he was such a renowned military general of unprecedented honor that exploits of his life became exaggerated to the point where he gained a mythic status across all of China, which was further cemented by him being a prime figure in one of the literary prize jewels in the canon of Chinese classical literature: *Romance of the Three Kingdoms*.

In life and in legend, Guan Yu epitomized all that is celebrated about Litha and of honorable masculinity. He was powerful but never oppressive, using his strength to protect the weak. He was honest and a man of his word, assertive in his statements but never aggressive. He was a beacon of bright hope and optimism to his men without being false or promising more than he could assure. And he was known to be particularly handsome and strong in body without being vain and always made sure to balance his physical strength with academic intelligence and philosophic openness to wonder. If humankind saw the verdant strength of the earth in its prime so strongly during Litha that we made it the standard for paradise's perfection, so, too, did Guan Yu set the standard for ideal masculinity that all men should strive to be at all times.

However, as great and admirable as Guan Yu was, his belief in his own virtues and prowess served to be his undoing. In summertime, the sun is at its visual peak, but the brighter it shines, the less you can actually see, since with its radiance come blinding glares and the need to squint in order to perceive. So, too, was Guan Yu's own radiating brilliance. In a case of positivity turning toxic, he believed that all soldiers were as honorable as him (or at least strived to be) and that his supreme power and martial ability equated to invincibility. As a result, Guan Yu blinded himself to the fact that his allies were conspiring to betray him. Thus, self-delusion about his inability to lose or be captured led to his capture and, ultimately, his execution.

Like Guan Yu, the vibrancy and splendor of the earth in her prime season of Litha is ideal but blinding in its brightness. So, too, are all the primes of life. When we are in our prime, whether it be in regard to youth, career, ability, and so forth, we have the self-blinding human tendency to believe it'll last forever, that this is how it'll always be. The pains and debilitations of old age are too alien to truly comprehend for twenty-somethings just maturing into adulthood. Success at our job breeds the logical belief that more successes are to come, and we cannot imagine a sudden merger or downsizing that could lay us off this time next year. And when we first enter into a new romance with someone who makes us feel as if no one in history has ever known such a love before, the thought of a bitter breakup or viciously litigious divorce seems impossible because we are so certain in this prime moment that this love will last forever and endure all things. Alas, nothing lasts forever, and not even the prime season of Litha or the mighty paragon of war-riorship Guan Yu are invincible.

Nevertheless, this prime of warmth and paradisiac splendor is meant to be enjoyed. We must enjoy the weather and sunshine while it's here, youth while we have it, the job while we're suc-ceeding, and love while it lasts. To be fatalistically focused on the ephemerality of these seasons of life is to not enjoy them and to never get to experience them at all. The trick is to hold on loosely. Grasp the moment at hand but never clutch. Like water, the more tightly we try to hold on to it, the faster it slips out of our hands. But if we cup our palms and hold our hands open, we can have more for longer, albeit not forever. Much like life, these prime moments are special *because* they're fleeting. So, enjoy the sunshine, just don't let it blind you to the future.

Feasts and Treats

Nathan M. Hall

THE SUMMER SOLSTICE FEELS like a great excuse for a classic warm-weather party. These recipes encapsulate the energy of the longest day of the year, celebrating all the light before the days start to become shorter again.

Pulled Pork

There's nothing that feels more lazy and summery than spending the afternoon minding something slowly cooking for dinner.

Prep time: 20 minutes
Cooking time: 3 hours
Servings: 8–10

3–4 pounds pork butt, bone removed
Pork rub seasoning
    2 tablespoons paprika
    1½ tablespoons brown sugar
    1 tablespoon kosher salt
    1 tablespoon chili powder
    1 tablespoon ground cumin
    1 tablespoon granulated garlic
    1 tablespoon onion powder

1½ teaspoons mustard powder

1½ teaspoons black pepper

1½ teaspoons ground celery seed

½ teaspoon cayenne

2 tablespoons peanut or other neutral oil

1 large sweet onion, peeled, cut in half, and sliced

1 can of beer, a lager or whatever you have on hand that
    you actually like

1 tablespoon apple cider vinegar

Potato rolls or hamburger buns

Pickle spears

Your favorite hot sauce, BBQ sauce, or mustard sauce

You can cheat and make this in a pressure cooker in a fraction of the time, but I prefer the low and slow method using a Dutch oven or other oven-safe pot that has a tight-fitting lid. One other suggestion that I won't get into here is to smoke the pork butt in your smoker or grill for a couple hours before transferring to the Dutch oven.

For this recipe, start by preheating the oven to 275°F. Cut the pork butt into 5 or 6 roughly equal pieces. Combine all of your pork rub seasonings and rub it in really well with the meat. Take the rub by the handful and work it into every corner and crevice. Place the Dutch oven on a burner on the stove over medium-high heat. Once a drop of water quickly evaporates, pour in the peanut oil and then place the chunks of pork in. Let sear for about two minutes before turning with tongs until all sides have a nice browned color and the seasoning has seared into the meat. Remove the meat and place the onion in the bottom of the pan, cooking until they just begin to go translucent, scraping up any browned bits from the meat with a wooden spatula. Add in the beer and apple cider vinegar and return the pork to the pot. Some people add barbeque sauce or ketchup at this point, but I like to keep additions minimal so that the flavor of the meat really shines through. There's plenty of time for doctoring it up once it's done. Place the lid on and move it into the oven.

Let the aroma fill the house for the next 3 hours or so. A kitchen thermometer should read 205°F when it's ready to come out of the oven. If it's not there yet, just set a timer for another half hour and keep repeating until you've hit that temperature. What's so special about 205°F? That's when all of the fats and connective tissues have dissolved and mingled with the meat, giving it the classic pulled pork flavor.

When it's ready, pull it out of the oven and let it rest with the lid off for about 15 minutes. Transfer the meat and onions to a large bowl and using two forks (or your hands, if it's not too hot) begin pulling apart the chunks of meat. It will mostly come apart in long strands, no need to shred it.

When you're ready to serve, put a pickle on a bun and top it with a generous portion of the pork. Eat it plain or with your favorite sauce on top.

Fennel and Citrus Salad

A perfect complement to the rich and savory pulled pork sandwiches, this bright salad is a perfect palate cleanser.

Prep time: 25 minutes

Servings: 4–6

2 tablespoons white wine vinegar
1 shallot clove, thinly sliced
1 teaspoon sea salt
4 tablespoons olive oil
1 tablespoon honey
2 fennel bulbs, cut in half, cored and sliced thin, fronds reserved
1 orange, cut (see instructions)
1 red grapefruit, cut (see instructions)
5-ounce package baby spinach
1 cup Castelvetrano olives, halved
Parmigiano-Reggiano cheese, thinly sliced

Start the dressing in a small bowl by adding the white wine vinegar, shallot, and sea salt. Swish around to mostly cover the shallot and allow to macerate for about 10–15 minutes. Add the olive oil and honey and mix well.

Prepare the fennel as instructed and place into a large bowl. Pour about half of the dressing over it, and gently massage the fennel to briefly macerate.

Cut just the very top and bottom off of the orange and grapefruit and make a slice down one side of each to loosen the peel, rotating as you remove it with your fingers. Remove any white pith that was left behind. Break the orange into segments and add to the fennel. Divide the grapefruit and, using a paring knife, cut down the white lines between each segment and carefully remove the fruit. Place into the bowl.

When ready to serve, place baby spinach into a serving bowl, top with remaining half of the dressing, tossing to incorporate, followed by the fennel and fruit. Add olives and cheese and tear up some fronds of fennel, sprinkle over the top, and serve.

Baked Beans

My palate is less geared toward sweet things, so my baked beans are more similar to British-style beans rather than American Southern style. There's still some sweetness, but it's balanced by the vinegar and the saltiness of the broth.

Prep time: 10 minutes
Cooking time: 30 minutes–1 hour
Servings: 8

Olive oil
1 small yellow onion, sliced thin
3 14-ounce cans white kidney beans (aka cannellini beans)
1 cup chicken or vegetable broth
1 6-ounce can tomato sauce
1 tablespoon tomato paste
¼ cup apple cider vinegar

1 tablespoon Dijon mustard

2 tablespoons brown sugar

1 teaspoon garlic powder

1 teaspoon onion powder

½ teaspoon fresh ground black pepper (just a few turns on your pepper mill)

Kosher salt as needed

Warm a pot on the stove and pour in enough olive oil to coat the bottom of the pan. Add onions and a sprinkle of salt, cook until they just start to become translucent, and then add all the remaining ingredients. Stir and bring to a boil before reducing to a simmer over low heat, leaving uncovered.

Allow beans to gently simmer in the pot for 30 minutes to an hour. When the sauce thickens up and has reduced by about a third, they will be ready to serve.

Quick-Pickled Cucumber and Red Onion

Alternately known as *refrigerator pickles*, I still remember the zing of vinegar that turned unappealing cucumbers into a must-have snack on warm days.

Prep time: 10 minutes

Cooking time: Overnight

Servings: 6–8

1 cup white vinegar

1 cup water

1–2 teaspoons sea salt

1 English cucumber, sliced

1 red onion, peeled and halved, cut into thin wedges

1 teaspoon mustard seeds

1 teaspoon peppercorns

In a large bowl with a sealing lid, pour in the vinegar, water, and one teaspoon of salt. Mix well and taste. Adjust as needed; it should taste vinegary and a bit briny. Add in cucumber, onion, mustard seeds, and peppercorns. Close lid tightly and put in the refrigerator at least overnight.

The cucumbers and onions should be softened but still crisp and have a delicious vinegar tang. The mustard seeds and peppercorns will add a more nuanced flavor profile by the second day. Transfer to a large Mason jar to save space in the refrigerator if you like. These are great as a little salad or served on the pulled pork sandwiches.

You can also experiment with other ingredients to tweak the flavor; some ideas include red pepper flakes, garlic cloves (they turn blue in vinegar, which can be kind of cool), sugar, dill seeds, dill fronds, coriander seeds, etc. I've even seen people use clove buds in their pickles, but that can be an acquired taste.

Crafty Crafts

Raechel Henderson

MIDSUMMER SEES THE LONGEST day and the shortest night of the year. Sitting opposite of Yule, the energy of the sabbat is full of the sun's potency, grounding, vibrancy, and certainty. The year is at the halfway mark; all the hard work was done during the previous months, and now is the time to rest and relax. Of course, when it comes to crafting, we don't really relax; there's always something to be made, some chore to be done, or some recipe to cook. But Midsummer efforts lack the urgency of sowing and planting or harvesting and preserving. We can take a moment to breathe a deep sigh of relief and just be. Make up a batch of incense cones to use in the coming months as you work other spells and rituals. Formed during the abundant energy of Midsummer, they'll bring certainty and clarity to you when you burn them later on.

DIY Incense Cones

For most of human history, incense has been used the world over in religious and lay ceremonies. Incense cones are a mixture of dried, ground plant material and a binding agent like makko powder. Makko comes from the bark of the *tabu-no-ki* tree (Japanese bay tree). The bark is powdered and used in both cone and stick incense. It has very little scent of its own so that the herb matter you add to the cones will be allowed to shine through. You can get makko powder from various online retailers.

When deciding on which herbs to include in your incense cones, think about what properties you want to bring into your space. Do you enjoy certain scents more than others? There's no point in making incense out of peppermint if you don't like the smell of it, for example. Choose herbs that you can easily source, whether that be from the grocery store, your garden, or even just your spice rack. There's nothing wrong with picking up ground ginger from your local market to use in incense cones.

Make sure the plant matter you are using is safe to burn. The smoke should not be toxic to you or your pets. Also, only burn your incense cones in a fireproof container. I use a cast iron cauldron in which I have a small pile of sand to help disperse the heat. Finally, never leave incense to burn unattended.

You might even want to make a mix of herbs for your incense cones. For example, you might mix ground mugwort, catnip, and thyme together in a cone that is used to encourage prophetic dreams. Or add ground allspice and nutmeg together to create a cone to burn to increase your luck. Rose, lavender, and violet petals can be dried and ground and mixed together for a cone to burn when you are casting love spells. Once you start experimenting with different herbs and combinations, the possibilities are endless.

Materials

3 tablespoons of dried, ground plant matter
1¼ tablespoon makko powder
Water

Tools

Measuring spoons
Bowl
Whisk
Eyedropper

Parchment paper

Water, or hydrosol

Optional: mortar and pestle or spice grinder

    Cost: $10–$15

    Time spent: 30 minutes to make the cones; 24–48 hours to dry them

Instructions

Start by creating sacred space in a manner set out by your path. Next, grind your dried plant matter into a powder if it isn't already. You can use your mortar and pestle to start the process and finish it in a spice grinder. The material doesn't have to be a fine powder; if there are little bits of herb that are larger, your incense cone will still work, but you want to get the herbs as small as possible. You will want to mix your ground plant material with the makko powder. Use a whisk to ensure that the two powders mix thoroughly.

Using an eyedropper, add a little bit of water at a time to make a dough. You can also use hydrosol instead of water if you have that on hand. As you are adding the water, consider the fact that you are mixing elements of earth and water together to end up with a cone that will incorporate the fire and air elements. Think about how this alchemy changes materials from one to another. Think about Midsummer—how it is the halfway point in the year. But that shouldn't mean the year is half gone; instead, you have the rest of the year to change yourself if you wish.

Knead your dough so that all the dry ingredients are moist. Use a ½ teaspoon to scoop out some of the dough. Shape it into a long and narrow cone and set it on the parchment paper. You should be able to make 4–6 cones from the dough.

Let the cones dry for twenty-four to forty-eight hours. Halfway through the drying time, turn the cones on their side so the bottoms can dry.

Store your incense cones in a tightly closed container. Make sure to label them with the ingredients, magical correspondences, and

date you made them so that you know which are which. You might even make a note of what you intend to use them for just so you aren't faced with a container full of incense cones and no idea when to use them.

To use your incense cones, set them in a heatproof container. Light the top of the cone and let the flame go out. It should smolder and smoke, releasing the scent into the air.

If you are having issues with your cones, like if they don't continue to burn after the flame goes out, try these fixes:

1. Your cones might be too big and so proper airflow isn't happening. To counter this, when you make your cones, use a toothpick to poke a hole through the cone. This will allow air to be drawn up from the bottom and through the cone, feeding the cone's ember.

2. You might need to add more makko powder to your dough. Increase the amount of makko powder by ¼ of a teaspoon to the incense cone mix until you have reached the right ratio for a smooth burn.

3. Your cones might not be completely dry. Make sure you are allowing them a full forty-eight hours to dry completely, especially if you are in a humid climate.

Litha Meditations

Elizabeth Barrette

SUMMER BRINGS THE HEIGHT of activity. Litha celebrates light at its peak. This is a great time for outdoor mindfulness, such as forest meditations. You can also use meditation to support your goals, as with positive affirmations. Explore some different approaches to each and see what works for you.

Forest Meditations

Today, more people live in urban environments surrounded by human-made things than in rural or wilderness environments surrounded by nature. Since humans evolved in nature, this separation from proper habitat can cause problems. Forest meditations have developed as a way to reconnect with nature and make a short visit more effective.

Nature-deficit disorder is an umbrella term for all the bad things that happen when humans get stuck in artificial environments too long. These include exhaustion, irritation, attention issues, anxiety, depression, technological dependencies, relationship problems, tired eyes, sleep disturbances, and other complaints. They all stem from feeling overworked and disconnected. Forest meditations help the mind and body to slow down, relax, and reconnect.

Mindfulness helps contain a wavering mind and quell unhelpful thoughts. It reduces negative feelings like fear and anger while increasing positive ones like peace and happiness. It boosts self-awareness, self-worth, and confidence. Nature aids metabolic health, the immune system, and organ functions. It lowers stress, burnout, and muscle tension. This improves quality and duration of sleep. By filling your energy reserves, it raises your ability to resist cravings and bad habits—your "won't-power" (Collins 2017). In this calm space within, you may find answers for key questions and make better choices. All of these things contribute to better connections, interactions, and relationships with other people.

There are multiple types of forest meditations. The most popular, walking mindfully through the trees, is also called *forest bathing.* Find a woodland that buffers the noise and smells of urban life. Begin by breathing in the clean forest air and noticing its smells—the rich earth, green leaves, or flowers that may be blooming. As you walk, feel the ground underfoot. Is it packed dirt, sandy, gravel, springy moss, crunchy leaves? Listen to the sounds as the forest breathes with you: birds calling and leaves whispering. Look at the countless shades of green. Imagine that you are soaking in the life energy all around you. Let go of everything that bothers you and just be. Remember that it's not about controlling your thoughts but rather ensuring that your thoughts don't control you.

Another option is a beauty walk. As you travel along the trail, look for things that are lovely, such as a flower, a colorful leaf, or an interesting stone. Find things ahead of you and on either side of you, which pass behind you as you walk. Beauty surrounds you on all sides. The more you wrap yourself in beauty, the harder it gets to feel downhearted, because beauty lifts you up.

For a seated meditation, examine the small things around you. Some trees like oaks support hundreds or even thousands of other species. See the moss on the ground, the lichens on trees or rocks. Watch ants or other insects going about their tiny lives. The forest floor is a whole little ecosystem of its own.

Do a life energy meditation by focusing on all the lives around you. Visualize each one as a point of light, glowing like a firefly. Imagine them connected by shining threads to each other and to you. A forest is a living network, and in this moment, you are part of it.

Positive Affirmations

Positive affirmations are like mantras you create for yourself. They are simple statements about what is now, what is developing, or how you want to view yourself. By focusing on constructive rather than destructive ideas, you attract more of what you want and less of what you don't. This meditation helps you shape your thought patterns and practices. Consider how to make and choose good affirmations.

First, affirmations only work when you *believe* them. If you try one that isn't true for you, it won't work. So you have to find phrases that feel right to you in the present moment. You can start with a "next step" affirmation and move up to better ones later.

Second, the subconscious doesn't grasp negatives well. If you say "no fear," then what it hears is "fear." They're called "positive" affirmations because you have to frame the concept in terms of what you want rather than what you prefer to avoid.

Third, pay attention to time frame. This touches on belief but also on self-sabotage. If you say something like "I am" when it's not true yet, then it won't work. (Some people feel that "fake it till you make it" works; others find that it backfires. In my experience, plausible affirmations work better.) So if you say something like "I will be," then it may get stuck in the future and never manifest. Terms like "may" and "could" give you some wiggle room. Terms like "becoming," "improving," "increasing," and so on are powerful because they propel you along a path of growth.

You can use positive affirmations in many different meditative techniques. One way is as a mantra, which you repeat over and over to focus your meditation. Another is as a reminder. For instance, you might hang a poster with your affirmation on the wall so that whenever you see it, you are reminded of your meditative focus and your calm mind. This is why mantra wall hangings are so popular: they extend the benefits of meditation beyond an actual session. You can also use affirmations as stepping stones that mark your path of personal growth. As they change, you can see how far you have come. Positive phrases become part of your self-talk and help maintain healthy thought patterns.

To meditate with positive affirmations, first choose a phrase. Sit comfortably. Take a few deep breaths to relax. Bring your attention to your breath. Then focus on your positive affirmation. You can gaze at written words, repeat them silently, or say them aloud. Concentrate on the meaning and visualize them manifesting.

Here are some positive affirmations to try:

- "I am right where I need to be in this moment."
- "Today I choose to be kind to myself."
- "I can do hard things."
- "With every breath, I become calmer."
- "I am learning and growing."
- "My skills overcome my challenges."
- "I appreciate the good things in my life."
- "I connect myself with the world around me."
- "Today, I embody my best self."
- "In this moment, I choose fun and playfulness."
- "I make time to follow my inspiration."
- "I honor my body right now."
- "I move with grace and intention."
- "Relaxation is constructive."
- "Peace begins with me."
- "Be here now."

Summer is the season of growth. Affirmations and outdoor meditations help you expand your awareness and appreciate the world around you.

Resource

Collins, Clare. "9 Ways 'Won't-Power' Is Better Than 'Willpower' for Resisting Temptation and Helping You Eat Better." The Converstion. January 12, 2017. https://theconversation.com/9 -ways-wont-power-is-better-than-willpower-for-resisting -temptation-and-helping-you-eat-better-71267.

Litha Ritual

Emma Kathryn

LITHA IS THE PERFECT time for rituals, spells, and workings that focus on harnessing the solar power that abounds on the longest day and the benefits it brings to us. Litha is a time to take stock, to see things with the clarity of the midday sun so that we can direct the life-giving and life-promoting energies into our own dreams and ambitions, making them manifest into concrete realities.

Harness the Power of the Sun

This spell is designed to tap into the energies of Litha and direct them into desires and goals that you have already been working so hard toward. It also encompasses the need to see things with clarity in a rested and calm way by helping us to connect with the land where we live. It's also a fantastic way to incorporate the tarot into your witchcraft practice in a unique way, making these mystical little cards more than just a divination system.

For this ritual, you will need

A white or yellow candle to represent the sun (a tealight candle is perfectly fine)

Lighter or matches

The Sun tarot card (or an image of it)

234

Pen and paper
Fireproof dish or cauldron

This spell also includes a short visualisation. You may find it helpful to make a voice recording of it (on your phone or computer is just fine). Alternatively, you can read the visualisation a couple of times and simply go for it!

If you wish to prepare the ritual area first, then simply making sure the space is tidy and somewhere you are unlikely to be disturbed is perfectly fine, though you can be as elaborate as you like. And the same goes for yourself too! If you prefer to have a ritual bath or shower, then go for it, but alternatively, simply washing your hands and face is adequate.

When you are ready, gather all of your items and place them in your working area. Make sure you have enough room to sit comfortably, allowing yourself a few moments to settle. You can sit on a chair or on the floor in whatever position suits you best.

Meditation

When you are ready, light the candle. Watch the light and flame shift as it catches the gentle air currents of your surroundings. Pass your hand above the flame so that the heat gently warms your hand. Feel its power, its energy.

Now take the tarot card and hold it or place it so that your gaze sits comfortably on it. Take in all the details of the card—the colours, the imagery. Lose yourself in the details until they take on a life of their own. Daydream on the card. Imagine you can feel the heat of the sun in the card, the joy of the beings shown. Feel the brightness and energy of the card. Let time pass. How long? Who knows. Perhaps it feels like two minutes—five or ten even. It matters not, only the immersion into the card. If you struggle with this part, then perhaps focus on one part of the card before shifting your gaze on to the next and the next. Or you might simply decide to focus on the colours and the feelings and sensations they invoke within you.

Power of the Litha Sun Visualisation

Now it is time for a short visualisation that will help channel all of those thoughts, feelings, and ideas from the card meditation into energy for your spell. If you have made a recording of the visualisation, then now is the time to press play.

Close your eyes. Perhaps you can see the afterimage of the flame from your candle, or perhaps the gentle reds behind closed lids hint at light and warmth and energy. Allow yourself a moment to just relax. Let your breathing come naturally, simply paying attention to sensations as they arise and subside within your body.

Feel the substance of your seat supporting you, and allow your body to relax further. This is the time of Litha, the time for luxurious rest. There's no rush on this, the longest day. Acknowledge sounds outside of the room. Bring that attention closer now, paying attention to sounds within the room, simply noticing them as they arise. Bring your attention inward even more, focusing on the sensations within the body, the expansion of the ribs and chest as you inhale, perhaps clenching and unclenching different muscles or feeling the relaxation spread through your body.

Take a deep breath and hold for a count of four…three…two…one…and release, allowing your breathing to return to normal. As you do, see yourself in a place that is familiar to you, perhaps a garden, park, mountain, or beach. It can be somewhere real that is meaningful to you or a place of your imagination. See yourself there at Litha. It is midday and no clouds are in the sky. The sun is warm, pleasantly so, and high in the sky, chasing away all shadows and doubt. You feel strong and confident. See yourself standing there, soaking up the sun and all it has to offer. Feel power, abundance, clarity, and energy flow into you, and yet you feel rested and energised all at the same time. Soak in this energy, taking as much time as you need—for this is Litha, the longest day, and time is of no concern. This is your time. Feel yourself fill and pulse with power and energy, with confidence and clarity.

When you have taken your fill of solar energy, take a deep breath, holding for a count of four…three…two…one…Open your eyes.

Power of the Litha Sun Spell

Now it is time for the spell.

On your paper, write down what it is you want to achieve, being as specific as possible, and then fold the paper. Hold the paper to the candle until it catches fire and then place in the cauldron or fireproof dish, saying:

> *Power of the Litha sun,*
> *Strengthen that which I have begun.*
> *Let me relish in victories won.*
> *And let me see clearly what still must be done.*
> *Let my efforts grow, strengthen, and bloom,*
> *Ready for reaping at the harvest soon.*
> *Power of the Litha sun,*
> *As I will it, my spell is done!*

When the paper has burned away, making sure the fire is completely spent and no embers are left, take the ashes outside and throw them into the air, letting any swirls of air catch them and carry them away, letting your ambitions, goals, and aims take foot in the world, ready to grow, bloom, and manifest into reality!

Notes

Lammas

Join the Dance of Death

Ben Stimpson

WHILE IN THE WESTERN calendar we are used to seeing autumn as starting in September or even October in the Northern Hemisphere, traditionally, many societies marked the beginning of the autumn as the first harvest. This was the festival popularly called *Lammas* or *Lughnasadh* in Wicca and Neopaganism but traditionally named Hlāfmæsse, Loaf Mass, Lughnasadh, Lammastide, Gŵyl Awst, etc. Throughout August, there are other harvest celebrations or observances to gain blessings for the work ahead. It is a time of activity, work, and community. And if we look at the year as the life cycle of the world, it is also a time of middle age and the journey toward the grave.

The Harvesttime—Bounty, Prosperity, and Death

I think we can see some friction between viewing the cycles of nature through a solar lens and through a chthonic lens in the symbolism of these holidays. While the two impact each other, they exist on slightly different timelines. The solstices of the Wheel of the Year mark important points of solar energy in the year, but the cross quarters each represent the start of the change of the seasons. The various feasts in the Northern Hemisphere around this time of year traditionally celebrate the first reaping of the harvest and the influx of new food as the previous year's stocks begin to run dry. Before the age of supermarkets, people were at the mercy of agrarian cycles. Planning had to happen to save enough food to survive the rest of the year. After surviving the winter, sowing the crops, tending them, and watching them grow, the first harvest is the gleeful time of completing the cycle and starting again. Over the next three or four months, communities engaged in heavy communal labour to bring in the harvest and celebrate this plenty. It was a time of work but also a time to deepen social cohesion and bonding. The various harvest festivals through this period are all about sustenance, prosperity, and *life*. At the end of the harvest, communities sighed deeply in thanksgiving for a bounty that would (hopefully) sustain them until the next year.

While death is not a focus of these festivals, death does have an important role to play, and I believe it is here that death can be honoured and remembered for its ever-present role. It is precisely because of the cyclical nature of these energies that death is both an ending and the beginning.

Let's look at it from an energetic point of view by backtracking to the previous year and understanding what brought us to this place. The traditional agrarian cycle is spring (sowing seeds), summer (growing), autumn (harvest), and then winter (stasis). This is truly a cyclical relationship, not linear. The dying off during the previous harvest leads to the seeds that grow again. That's it; that's the nature of life. That's what we celebrate when we harvest—we celebrate the life-giving properties of the food we just reaped, but we also celebrate the natural and important ingredient of death in that process.

This natural cycle is our own life cycle, because for me, aside from the festivity and joy of bounty, it is this understanding of imminent and eventual death that begins to dawn on all of us, especially as we reach an age of maturation. Death can strike at any time, and we see that throughout the year as plants fail to grow and disease and blight strike. But, for those of us who survive to the period of harvest, we see in ourselves the maturation, and we are the ones who get to enjoy the fruits of the labour of last year's harvest and the sowing of the seeds earlier in the year.

For many Neopagans and witches, we don't live in an agrarian society anymore, but we do live in a seasonal world where the tilt of the earth will impact the flora of wherever we live. The more northern or southern you live, the more dramatically these changes will be seen. This annual cycle is often celebrated through the imagery of John Barleycorn, the spirit of the harvest, who is carefully collected and protected during the winter, ready to be reborn again into the land the next spring. John Barleycorn is a potent spirit of this time of year, but that spirit's journey is not necessarily our own journey or relationship to this season. To explore our relationship to alternatives to John Barleycorn, I'd like to guide us to other stories.

The Historiola of the Three Living and the Three Dead

The following story and ritual are constructed as a historiola of three separate traditional European folktales, each of which I believe fits well with the energy of this time of year. The stories are that of the "Three Living and the Three Dead," "The Mowing Devil," and the "Danse Macabre" ("Dance of Death").

Historiola is a modern term applied to the formation of rituals (or spells, charms, and curses) heavily informed by and connected to a specific closed narrative, deriving logic, symbolism, and power from that story. The crucial distinction between historiola-type rituals and others also informed by story is that the ritual (or spell, charm, or curse) incorporates the narrative directly as opposed to peripherally. This is achieved by referencing the story in the performance of the ritual. What becomes important to the power of the ritual is not necessarily all the elements of the original narrative being present, but instead evoking the story by recitation or mention of a key scene.

A very widespread form of historiola is the so-called Merseburg charms found in various versions throughout northern Europe over the past thousand or more years. The older form of one of the charms evoked a story of the gods Oðinn and Baldr going on a ride, one of their horses breaking its leg, and Oðinn healing the break. The versions of the charm derived from this story combined the recitation of a stanza of the scene where Oðinn bound the horse's leg with some ritual action mimicking the one he performs. The Merseburg charms eventually evolved to adapt Christian symbolism, where Oðinn became replaced by Jesus.

An example of a non-historiola ritual that is informed by story is the Christian Lammastide ritual of taking bread to the church, which derives from a story of God commanding Moses to bring a sheaf of wheat into the temple so that a priest may wave it for the Lord (Leviticus 23:10–13). This action does not necessarily include an evocation of that particular passage of the Bible, as the story is prescriptive of what actions must be taken.

As we look to celebrate our feast through ritual, let us begin with a story…

Once upon a time, three hunters gathered one morning to go out for a hunt. By midday, the three had travelled far into the forest, and they'd had no luck finding any game. They turned back and came to a solitary lane, and stood before them in the road were three corpses. The three living hunters and the three corpses stared at each other, the hunters filled with revulsion and fright. One of the corpses stepped forward. Its face was skeletal with bits of decayed flesh clinging to it, and it began to laugh heartily. A second corpse stepped forward, and just like the first, its face was decomposing. Worms were wriggling through the holes where its nose had once been, and the deep eye sockets that once had been eyes stared blankly. It gave a low, silent bow. The third corpse, this one less decomposed than the first two, fixed the remainder of its eyes onto each of the men and began wailing as if sobbing in misery and pleading.

The three hunters were frozen in fright, for never had they encountered such a sight before. One of them said, "I am afraid!" Another said, "What is this trickery?" The third said, "Begone foul spirits!"

In unison, the three corpses spoke: "Listen here for what we say is truth. Just as you are now, so too were we…and just as we are now, so too will you be." The three corpses each introduced themselves as who they were when alive, and each one reflected the living hunter before them.

The one who had laughed said, "I was a learned scholar who knew so much and considered the world so seriously. Hiding away in my study, I never learned the sweetness of simple merriment. Now, I see all of existence as something to be joyful of and for!"

The second corpse, the somber one who bowed, said: "I was spontaneous and a daredevil in life, hot tempered and filled with passion. I flitted from one thing to another seeking fulfillment but felt empty. In death, I have learned the sweetness of peace and calm, and it nourishes my discarnate soul."

The third corpse, the one who wailed, said, "Unlike my companions, I have found no peace in death. I was a greedy farmer who hoarded my wealth. I told my labourers I would not pay them fairly, and that evening the Lord of the Harvest came to my fields and took all my grain as punishment. Now I wander, starving, and warning others."

All three in unison said, "Just as you are now, so too were we…and just as we are now, so too will you be!"

The three corpses offered to show the three living the cycles of life and death so they would not fear their time when it came. The three living followed the corpses off to a nearby field where a group of people were assembled surrounded by baskets of collected fruits and vegetables of the first harvest. A great scythe lay in the centre of the gathering, and as the three living watched, a tall figure strode into the circle followed by an entourage of spirits and dancing skeletons. This great figure was the Reaper, the Great Lord of the Harvest, whose scythe was used by the living to collect their crops. He had come to collect his due on behalf of the dead who worked so hard in life to create the harvest the living were about to enjoy.

The great figure took up his scythe, and his attendants went around the gathering collecting fruits from the living to take back to the realm of the dead. The three dead said to the three living that this gathering was the dance of death, a journey all living and all dead are continually on. "Just as you taste of the fruit, the vine begins to wither away," said the corpse who had been the farmer in life.

The assembled all linked hands and danced and sang in honour of the Lord of the Harvest. The great dance finished, the dead took up their baskets of offerings, and the Reaper led them away, inviting some of the members of the living who were themselves destined to die in the near future. The three living watched as this spectacle took place, and one of the corpses turned to them and said, "Do not mourn for the dead, for the dance never ends. We will return at the end of the harvest and dance together again."

The dead having departed, the living joined together in merriment and feasted, enjoying the first fruits of the harvest to come.

In my practice, the ancestors do not come just once a year; they are always present. But the latter half (or beginning half if you live in the Southern Hemisphere) of the year is a time of potency when dying and death are in focus. In our story, we are thanking the dead for their hard work during the previous cycles; their work led to our enjoyment of these fruits. We likewise acknowledge that this is the beginning of the dying half of the year, the half of the year of the dead. The Reaper is not just assisting to kick off the harvest time so the living can enjoy those fruits; the Reaper is also gathering the souls of those who have died and will die in the months to come, inviting all to join the danse macabre, the dance of death toward the grave. Whether we like it or not, just like the three living, we are all dying and we are all engaged in the dance. The dance of death is truly the dance of life, as all things are cyclical. At Samhain/Halloween, the dead will come dancing back again across the veil as ancestors to mark the end of the harvest season and to initiate the start of the death months.

Cosmic Sway

Michael Herkes

As the Wheel of the Year turns, we gather the first fruits of the harvest. Welcome to the season of Lammas, where we give thanks for nature's bounty and prepare for the coming autumn. This stretch of summer into early fall is packed with magical potential.

Observing Lammas

We kick off the month with Lammas on August 1. This sabbat is based on an ancient celebration of the first harvest. Now, I don't know about you, but for me, Lammas always feels like summer's last hurrah before we start that slow slide into autumn. It's a time to honor abundance, to give thanks for what we've grown (literally or metaphorically), and to start thinking about what we want to preserve for the colder months ahead.

For a simple Lammas ritual, try baking a loaf of bread from scratch. As you knead the dough, pour your intentions into it. What do you want to manifest in the coming season? What are you grateful for from the past year? When the bread is done, share it with loved ones or bury it outside as an offering to the land spirits. Alternatively, one of my favorite methods is to bury it in a garden, the woods, or an open field and allow the magic to be absorbed into the earth.

August Moon Magic

Now, let's talk Moon magic. August gives us two juicy lunar events to work with. First up, we've got a New Moon in Leo on August 12 at 1:37 p.m. Leo energy is all about confidence, creativity, and stepping into the spotlight. This is prime manifesting energy, folks. Write down your biggest, boldest dreams. Don't censor yourself. Then burn the paper, releasing those intentions to the universe. Just be careful—Leo energy can be a bit impulsive, so maybe sleep on any big decisions for a day or two.

For those of you who like to dress for magical success, Leo season is all about bold colors and statement pieces. Think gold jewelry, bright reds and oranges, or anything that makes you feel like royalty. It's not about showing off; it's about embodying your inner sovereign.

As we round out August, we're treated to a Full Moon in Pisces on August 28 at 12:18 a.m. Pisces energy is dreamy, intuitive, and deeply emotional. This is a great time for divination, dream work, or any kind of psychic development. You might want to try scrying with a bowl of water under the moonlight, or sleep with a piece of moonstone under your pillow to enhance prophetic dreams. Tap into the Pisces energy by wearing flowy fabrics, iridescent colors, and anything that makes you feel like a mystical sea creature. Shades of blue and green are perfect, and don't be afraid to add some sparkle.

September New Moon in Virgo and Uranus Retrograde in Gemini

On September 10, we've got a New Moon in Virgo at 11:27 p.m., coinciding with Uranus going retrograde in Gemini at 2:27 p.m. This retrograde is sticking around until February 8, 2027, so we're in for a long ride.

Uranus in Gemini is all about revolutionary ideas and communication breakthroughs. When it goes retrograde, it's like the universe is asking us to pause and reflect on how we share information and connect with others. You might find yourself questioning long-held beliefs or suddenly seeing things from a completely different perspective.

The New Moon in Virgo on the same day is like rocket fuel for this energy. Virgo is all about analysis, improvement, and practical magic. It's a perfect time to set intentions around how you want to grow and change over the coming months. Maybe you want to learn a new divination technique, start a magical journal, or finally organize your herb collection. Whatever it is, the Virgo New Moon will help you create a practical plan to make it happen.

For Virgo season fashion, think earthy tones and natural fabrics. Linen, cotton, and wool in shades of green, brown, and cream are perfect. Virgo energy is all about the details, so don't be afraid to accessorize with small, meaningful pieces—maybe a pendant with your favorite crystal or a bracelet woven with herbs.

Summary

Throughout this whole period, from Lammas to the edge of autumn, we're being called to balance opposing energies. We've got the fiery passion of Leo tempered by Pisces's watery depths. The practical earth magic of Virgo dances with Uranus's revolutionary air energy.

It's a powerful reminder that magic, like life, isn't about choosing one side or the other. It's about finding the balance, dancing between the elements, embracing both the earth beneath our feet and the stars above.

So as you move through this season, don't be afraid to explore all facets of yourself and your practice. Honor the harvest—your harvest, along with planting the seed of intention for the future. Start this season trusting your Leo-inspired confidence, but also listen to your Pisces intuition. Then, halfway through, do the practical, grounding work that Virgo calls for, but remain open to the revolutionary ideas Uranus might bring.

As we dance through Leo's fiery days into Virgo's earthy autumn, may your magic be strong, your intuition clear, and your spirit renewed. Here's to a season of growth, transformation, and cosmic adventures.

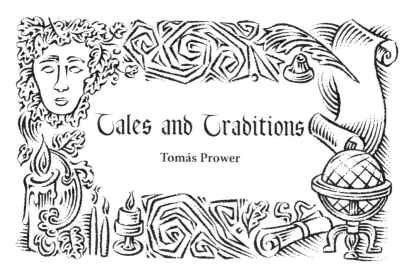

Tales and Traditions

Tomás Prower

Lammas (also often referred to as *Lughnasad* or *Lughnassadh*) is the first harvest sabbat of the year. While the other harvest sabbat of Mabon will have a bit more emphasis on sweet and luxurious corps (e.g., apples, grapes, wine, etc.) and a tinge of darkness that accompanies our preparation for the ascent of night and the coming coldness, Lammas has a stronger focus on life-sustaining staple foods, such as grains, and marking the official shift (physically and mentally) from growing to harvesting. However, the best harvests are never a surprise. As the old saying goes, "We reap what we sow," and life's surprises are only surprises if we're not paying attention during the early stages of sowing.

Amba/Shikhandi: A Hasty Harvest

In the *Mahabharata*, one of Hinduism's epic texts, there is one inspiring character whose story reflects the expectational harvest lessons of Lammas. Her name is Amba, and she had proposed marriage to a great and powerful warlord known as Bhishma. However, not only did Bhishma reject her as a wife and deem her unmarriageable, he did this in public, which was essentially a decree of doom to Amba's future prospects of marriage. Outraged, she sought revenge and began sowing the seeds to a harvest that would surprise her due to losing faith amid the "growing season" of her quest for vengeance.

Amba prayed to the destroyer god Shiva to one day be able to get her revenge, and his reply was both sobering and hopeful. He promised her that she would, indeed, attain her vengeance against the warlord Bhishma, but it would not be in this lifetime. Rather, he assured her that in her next reincarnation into this world, her vendetta would be successfully fulfilled. Right here is the moment in the story when Amba loses her way and ends up with a surprise harvest because the hatred and impatience to reap her vengeful harvest was so strong that it clouded her mind and her judgment. Hearing Shiva's promise, she immediately assumed that she would be reincarnated into a great and powerful young man who could take on an aging Bhishma in battle, and, wanting to rush things along, she killed herself so as to expedite reincarnating back into the world as this powerful man. She didn't know it then, but she was in for a big surprise.

Amba's prayers to Shiva had sown seeds of a very general nature that she wanted to manifest—that of vengeance. However, she expected a very specific way in which it would manifest despite not confirming that when the seeds were sown. Thus, Amba was extremely upset to realize that she had again reincarnated back into the world as a girl. Ironically, though, she was adopted by a powerful king who wanted a male heir but had none and who gave her the masculine name of Shikhandi. Amba (now known as Shikhandi) was more than happy to play along, thinking she'd fool her way to vengeance. Once again, she develops very specific expectations about her harvest despite forgetting how general she was in her intentions when sowing the seeds. However, she is eventually forced to marry, and her wife discovers the ruse, alerting her family and publicly shaming Shikhandi in this lifetime just as in the previous lifetime as Amba.

In Shikhandi's abysmal sorrow, a male nature spirit begins to feel profound empathy and offers to magically swap sexes with her. The legend continues from there, and Shikhandi ends up involved in the melee of an epic battle, wherein he finally gets to satiate his desire and reap the harvest he had sown when he brings about the demise of Bhishma.

Amba/Shikhandi's tale holds many lessons for us, but in regard to Lammas and reaping that which we sow, one of the biggest is being very specific in our magical intentions. We have to know exactly what we want to manifest in our future and have full faith in the Divine to manifest it, especially if the path toward manifestation isn't making sense in our limited, mortal minds. The beginning stages are always the most important. It's where foundations are built and expectations are set. If we plant rye, we should expect a harvest of rye and thus be better able to nurture and care for it in order to enable it to grow to its greatest abundance. But if we sow "food" and expect very specific types of food to be harvested, we may actually hinder its growth, nurturing it with care that may harm it.

Like Amba, if we are general in our intentions at the outset, we'll get a general manifestation. This is fine if we want general results, but if we want specific results, we must be clear about them in the beginning when we sow those seeds. Much of Amba's pain and anguish came from expecting and wanting very specific conditions to come about in a very accelerated timeline despite her general seeds of "vengeance" having been sown without specification or deadlines.

In regard to trusting the Divine, therein lied Amba's other self-induced frustration. She had a promise from Shiva himself. What more could she want? If we trust the Universe or whichever divinities we call upon to aid in our magic, we cannot suddenly lose faith in their assistance simply because things aren't going exactly as we had imagined. There are many routes to a single destination, and if we truly trust the Divine, if Amba had truly trusted Shiva with full faith, what matter is it that we are suddenly forced to take an unexpected detour or prevented from advancing for a little while as conditions farther down the road clear up? We must trust the powers and omniscient knowledge of the Universe, otherwise why call for their aid at all if we're just going to doubt them?

So this Lammas, look at the harvest you're reaping, and if it's not the harvest you had intended, go backward in time and see if you can spot when during the growing season you began to make specific expectations of seeds generally sown or if you even sowed the seeds you think you did. And also be sure that the seeds you are sowing now are those of things you wish to harvest. Then trust the Universe that the harvest will come, lest you sabotage it with doubt and specific expectations that were never confirmed during the sowing season.

Feasts and Treats

Nathan M. Hall

THE FIRST OF THE harvest festivals is usually too hot for much interest in working in the kitchen. These late-summer recipes will keep you cool and comfortable.

Harvest Bowl

Wheat berries are the fruiting body, so calling them berries is (kind of) appropriate! Generally, we use different parts of the fruit for making different kinds of flour, but whole wheat flour is made from the entire wheat berry.

Prep time: 30 minutes
Cooking time: 25 minutes
Servings: 6

2 cups wheat berries (sub buckwheat for a gluten-free alternative)
3 cups of water
Kosher salt
¼ cup ponzu (a traditional soy sauce mixed with citrus)
1 package extra-firm tofu, drained and cut into cubes
1–2 tablespoons cornstarch
1 bunch Swiss chard, stems removed
2 tablespoons rice wine vinegar

1 tablespoon honey

2 teaspoons chili garlic sauce

2 teaspoons sesame oil

1 radicchio, shredded

1 apple, cored and sliced (Granny Smith is a good variety for this.)

2 tablespoons toasted sesame seeds

Preheat the oven to 400°F.

If you're using hard wheat berries, rinse them and put into a saucepan with about 3 cups of water and a healthy pinch of salt. Bring to a boil and then reduce to a simmer. Put a lid on and let cook for about an hour.

While that's cooking, sprinkle some of the ponzu onto your tofu to marinate and then coat with a thin layer of cornstarch. Place prepared tofu onto a lined baking sheet and put in the oven for 25 minutes, turning halfway through.

Bring a pot of water to a boil and drop the Swiss chard in for about 3 minutes, until wilted. Drain the chard into a strainer and place into a bowl of ice water. Swish around until completely cooled and then strain again. Squeeze as much water as you can out of the chard and then roughly chop it on a cutting board and set aside.

Whisk the ponzu, rice wine vinegar, honey, chili garlic sauce, and sesame oil together in a bowl to make a sauce.

When the wheat berries are finished, drain off any excess liquid and mix in Swiss chard. Portion out into individual bowls for serving. Top with a sprinkling of shredded radicchio, a good helping of tofu, apple slices, and toasted sesame seeds. Drizzle a healthy serving of the sauce mixture over the top and serve.

Simple Mango Sorbet

Mangos are the fruit of the gods to me. Prior to living in Florida, I had never tasted one, but now I'm addicted. The grocery store versions leave a lot to be desired, but you can find passable diced mangoes in the freezer section.

Prep time: 5 minutes
Setting time: 1 hour or overnight
Servings: 4

2 16-ounce bags frozen mango chunks, or 4–5 medium-sized fresh
  mangos, peeled, pit removed, and cut into chunks and frozen
½ –1 cup maple syrup
3 tablespoons lime juice
Optional: 1 teaspoon Tajin seasoning, or more to taste

You can use a food processor or a blender for this recipe. Add frozen mango chunks to the food processor and drizzle over maple syrup, lime juice, and the Tajin seasoning to taste, if using.

Run the food processor to break up chunks, frequently opening the lid and scraping down the sides of the bowl. When the mixture is mostly smooth, adjust for taste as desired with more of the syrup, lime juice, or Tajin. Store in freezer to allow to set for at least 1 hour or overnight.

Honey Lemonade

Lammas is peak summer heat for me in Florida, and I know it stays pretty hot across most of the US at that time as well, so a refreshing drink is in order.

Prep time: 15 minutes
Cooking time: 3 minutes
Servings: 6 8-ounce servings

Bag of lemons
1 cup honey
5 cups water

Slice one lemon to float in the lemonade and use as garnishes. Juice the remaining lemons (it's not as labor intensive as you think) using a juicer and transfer to a carafe.

In a small pot, warm 1 cup of water until you start to see small bubbles form in the bottom. Remove from heat and pour in honey, stirring constantly until it dissolves. Top off with the remaining 4 cups of cold water and stir into the carafe containing the lemon juice. Serve over ice garnished with a twist of lemon.

Crafty Crafts

Raechel Henderson

ALSO KNOWN AS LAMMAS, Lughnasadh comes on August 1 and heralds the midway point between summer and fall. The energy of this sabbat is lush and vibrant and abundant. All the work we put into the summer months is paying off in a bountiful harvest that will see us through the dark of winter. It is a time of both endings, in the harvest of the wheat, and beginnings, when we start storing that harvest away. Even if you didn't sow a single row or can't keep a houseplant alive, you can still tap into the harvest energy with a pressed-flower suncatcher.

Pressed-Flower Suncatcher

Unlike the witch ball on page 296, which is meant to stop energies that might enter your home, the suncatcher helps to welcome in the energies of the flowers you use. Lughnasadh energy is one of flow—in and out. Just as the sun streams into our homes through our windows, the sun's light will flow through the suncatcher and power the energies of the flowers within.

You can pick up dried, pressed flowers from your local hobby store or make your own. Pressing the flowers is as easy as placing the blooms on wax paper and then stacking 4–6 heavy books atop them. In a week, they should be dry and flat enough for this craft. You can press a variety of flowers as well as leaves and individual petals. Take a walk in your neighborhood, a local park, or a nearby forest to gather your blooms. (Make sure you aren't gathering from private property unless you have permission.)

Choose flowers and plants that have properties you want to bring into your home. For example, use four-leaf clovers, ferns, oak, or holly leaves to create a suncatcher that will bring luck into your home. For a prosperity suncatcher, use chamomile, flax, goldenrod, maple or poplar leaves, or wheat heads. You can also choose flowers based on how they look to bring in general energies of beauty. Choose flowers such as daisies, pansies, lilacs, cosmos, marigolds, and zinnias for their vibrant colors and beautiful shapes. Don't be put off by the idea of using "weeds" either. Many wildflowers are classed as weeds solely because they grow wherever they please. The resilience and tenacity of those flowers can be especially useful in a home that is facing adversity.

You might even choose plants and flowers of all one color to engage in some color therapy. Blue flowers can be healing, green is linked to abundance and prosperity, red brings in passionate energies, while pink flowers are filled with loving vibrations. You don't have to use full flowers either. Dried petals and leaves can be arranged in mandalas for more meditative and contemplative energies.

This is a great craft to do with your children if you have any. It gives you the opportunity to introduce them to topics such as herbalism, the environment, and magic in a fun and hands-on way. Take a book on local wildflowers with you as you go out foraging with your children so that you can identify plants that you might not know by name. Let them pick out whatever flowers they want without thought about their properties. This allows children to start having confidence in their own creativity and magic.

Materials

Piece of blank paper
Embroidery hoop
Clear contact paper
Pressed flowers, leaves, and petals
Twine or ribbon

Tools

Scissors
Popsicle stick
Optional: tweezers

Cost: $10. The pressed flowers will be free unless you buy them. The embroidery hoop and the contact paper will be the most expensive materials for this project.

Time spent: 1 week to press the flowers if doing so, 30 minutes to make the suncatcher

Instructions

Create sacred space to work in according to your path. Take some time to plan how you want to arrange your pressed flowers. Lay the embroidery hoop on a piece of paper and trace the inside of it so you will know how much space you will have. Arrange your pressed flowers, leaves, and petals on the paper inside the circle. Once you are happy with your design, you can begin to transfer the flowers to the contact paper.

Cut two pieces of your contact paper into a circle that is larger than the embroidery hoop. Set one aside and peel off the backing of the other. Place the contact paper with the sticky side up. Lay the embroidery hoop gently on the contact paper so that you will be able to tell where to place your flowers. Using your fingers or tweezers, transfer the flowers from your paper template to the contact paper. Press gently to affix the flowers to the contact paper.

As you are working, consider the properties of the flowers you chose for this craft. Envision their energies being activated as the sunlight shines through the suncatcher and then filling your home. How will those energies affect your home? Will it feel different? Will the people inside act differently? What will be the outcome of hanging the suncatcher up?

Once you have placed down all the flowers, remove the hoop. Take the other circle of contact paper and remove its backing. With the sticky side down, place it over the flowers. Use the popsicle stick to press out any air bubbles and to secure the flowers.

Remove the inner circle from your embroidery hoop and place it under the contact paper with the flower design centered in it. Place the outer ring of the embroidery hoop over the inner circle, sandwiching the paper between the two. You may need to pull gently on the sides of the contact paper so that it is taut between the rings. Then tighten the screw at the top of the outer ring of the embroidery hoop to keep everything secure.

Hang the embroidery hoop in your window using twine or ribbon. Whenever your gaze is caught by the suncatcher, think about the energies that are coming into your house because of the flowers in it. See them swirling around your home, making it luckier, happier, and more loving.

Lammas Meditations

Elizabeth Barrette

By LATE SUMMER, THE weather tends to be sweltering and not much fun to go outside in. At Lammas, the crops are bursting with bounty, but not all of them are ready for harvest yet. This precarious time can feel oppressive or nerve-racking. This is a good occasion for meditations that give you a helping hand. An insight meditation can be done indoors or out using your senses. The ambient sound meditation is an indoor activity with music or nature sounds that you choose.

Insight Meditation

We experience the world through our senses. The physical senses are sight, sound, smell, taste, and touch. In mindfulness practice, the sixth sense is thought. What you experience can push you around if you don't stay centered. Insight meditation encourages you to observe what you perceive and then decide how to respond, or not, rather than just reacting automatically.

The goal of insight meditation is to understand the true nature of things and perceive them for what they really are. You must let go of preconceptions and judgments. Just accept each thing for itself. In this way, you come to observe things in your own life more accurately so that you can deal with them better. Say you hold a spoon as you cook and it gets too hot; then you know to let go of it. With practice, you can observe that a habit is causing you harm, and then you know to stop doing it. Mental clarity leads to right action. This fosters wisdom.

Imagine yourself as a room with five windows (your physical senses) and a door (your mental sense). Sitting in the middle, you can observe what happens at all of those openings. You could close the windows and door, shutting yourself in, but you don't have to. You could get up and run out through any of them, but you don't have to. Insight meditation is about sitting still, centered, noting what happens but not feeling compelled to act on it. You choose mindfully when to get up and do something.

For insight meditation, sit in a comfortable position. Breathe from your belly. Focus on the sensation of breathing. Next, turn your attention to touch and the other things you can feel. Note the floor or chair under you, your clothes against your skin, the temperature of the room, and so on. Set them aside as unimportant. Return your focus to your breath. Next, pay attention to what you hear. Listen for each sound, and name it as something you hear. Then set them aside and return to your breath. Focus on what you can smell. Note whether scents are pleasant or unpleasant. Then set them aside and return to your breath. Turn your attention to what you can taste. Perhaps there are flavors to go with the smells, or they may be different. Then set them aside and return to your breath. Consider what you can see. Look at the colors and shapes, then name the objects. Then set them aside and return to your breath. Finally, observe your thoughts. Note the ideas and beliefs that rise up in your mind. They may be helpful or unhelpful. Perceive them without judgment, only acceptance. Then set them aside and return to your breath.

When you meditate like this, you ground yourself in the here and now. It helps with all kinds of problems that disconnect you from your body or distract you with events of the past. It lets you choose mindfully how to respond instead of reacting thoughtlessly.

Sound Meditation

A sound meditation can use any kind of soothing background sound to promote calm and to cover background noise. Among the most popular options are nature sounds and mood music. In fact, they are often combined with soft music over a natural backdrop of sounds. It can create the sense of being outdoors even if you are inside because it is sweltering or pouring rain.

Most people meditate best in a peaceful environment. Noise can be very jarring and distracting. Complete silence is not ideal because it seems to magnify every tiny sound. This is why meditation gardens typically use trickling water or rustling leaves to create a baseline sound level. It covers minor noises and makes concentration easier. Ambient music or sound recordings accomplish the same effects.

This kind of meditation works well for beginners or for people struggling to meditate, because the soothing sound facilitates relaxation and lessens the tendency of boredom. It lowers cortisol and other stress chemicals in the body. It improves self-awareness, empathy, and the ability to manage challenges. Ambient music and nature sounds support your sense of rhythm and connection. Another advantage of recordings is that they provide a natural time frame for your practice, as the end of sound tells you when to stop. Even after a meditation session, you may find ongoing benefits in better memory and cognitive performance.

How do you choose a good soundtrack for your meditation? First, you have to like it or your subconscious will fight it. Second, suit the length of the track to your intended session length. It helps to keep a selection of shorter and longer tracks. Third, choose a slow rhythm. Your body will tend to match it, so pick something gentle and soothing. Next, pick soft instruments or nature sounds. Harp, flute, falling rain, and rustling leaves are all popular. Thrashing guitar or shrieking monkeys will not help you relax. Also consider whether you want a loose natural rhythm (like ocean waves), music with a long repeat, or neither. Too rigid a pattern makes it hard to unwind. Finally, suit the soundscape to your mental imagery and cultural context. If you imagine yourself on a tropical island, pick a rainforest or ocean soundtrack. If you set up your meditation space with Zen decor, consider *shakuhachi* or *koto* music.

For sound meditation, choose a place where you can play a recording without bothering anyone and without interruptions. Turn on your soundtrack. Sit in a comfortable position. Take a few deep breaths to relax. Focus your attention on your breath. Then shift your focus to the ambient sound. Listen deeply. What instruments do you hear? How do they interact? Can you hear animals or plants moving? What are they doing? Allow the sound to move over you and through you. Construct a mental image of the environment evoked by the sounds. Imagine yourself in that place, surrounded by the sounds. If other thoughts intrude, acknowledge them and then set them aside. Return your attention to the sound.

Pay attention to your insights and the sounds around you. Let them guide you through the season.

Lammas Ritual

Ben Stimpson

As THE FIRST HARVEST, the feast of the first week of August is a joyous time when the first fruits of the year are brought in and the harvest season commences. While this is a season of life and bounty, it is also a season of death, for as the old saying goes, you reap what you sow. The consequence of this bounty comes through the deaths of some of the plants that you have tended over the spring and summer. The relationship between life and death here is intimate, and if we see ourselves as the fruits of our ancestors' work, we too are on a journey to be harvested. In life, we can often delude ourselves into believing death is some far-away concept, but we are all always on the dance toward death. I invite you to celebrate this danse macabre (dance of death) through the following ritual.

The Dance of Life and Death

This Lammastide ritual is designed to be performed in a group, almost as a mummers dance or mystery play, but can also be completed individually at an altar space. This rite should be performed in the evening, but the late afternoon also works. I have included a version for both groups and individuals below.

What you will need

Prebaked cookies or biscuits in the shape of people (store bought is fine, but if baking yourself, include candied fruit and dried berries). None of these biscuits are to be eaten by the living.

Face paint in order to paint three people with skull paint, plus enough face paint for everyone attending.

Costume for the Reaper: skull mask, crown, dark clothing, and a hood.

A scythe or pitchfork (real or prop)

1–3 woven baskets (depending upon how many attendants are chosen).

1 tealight, other type of candle in safe holder, or lantern for everyone attending.

A lighter or matches.

A drum or pot that can be struck to create a beat.

Objects representing death and dying.

Donation of food for the food bank, such as tinned fruits and vegetables.

Optional: participants may bring an image of a recently departed loved one.

Preparation

This rite is designed to coincide with other Lammastide rites and is an honouring of death. The general time that's appropriate to conduct this ritual is late afternoon or early evening. Before meeting, either purchase or bake people-shaped cookies. If you do bake your own, select your favourite recipe and add into the dough mixture candied fruit and dried berries to represent the first fruits. These cookies are not to be eaten by the living. They will eventually be given over to the representatives of the dead to take back with them to the realm of the dead as their share of the first fruits.

Find a space, whether inside or outside, where your group can gather. If this is the only ritual you are performing, tie it in with a potluck or communal feast and decorate the space to reflect the dawn of the harvest period. A large area in the centre of the space will need to be clear for a communal circle dance, and so place any tables off to the side.

The "altar space" for this ritual is not an ancestor altar; it is a *memento mori* altar. A *memento mori* is an artistic expression of the concept of the inevitability of death. Attendees of the ritual are encouraged to bring a symbol that represents death and dying with them to place onto the memento mori as an embodiment of the passage of time, dying, and the looming reality of death. Objects here could include sand hourglasses, clocks, skulls, cut flowers that are wilting, books or poems on death, coffin shapes, or other such symbols representing death. If in your area any trees have begun to drop their leaves, collect those leaves and place them onto the memento mori too. In this case, it is not advisable to place images of the dead on this altar, as the celebration of the ancestors is at Samhain. The point of this ritual is to offer the Reaper and the dead their share of the first fruits and to honour the livings' place in the danse macabre. It's not meant to dwell on honouring the dead specifically.

Traditionally, the direction of death and the afterlife for many traditions has been the west or north, and so place the memento mori on either a small table or as a display on the floor in the north or west corner. In the very centre of the space, place the scythe or pitchfork.

Group Ritual: The Danse Macabre and Reaping of the Harvest

If numbers allow, select attendees to play the following roles: the Reaper and the Three Dead. If there are not enough members, the Reaper and a single attendant will suffice. The Reaper is encouraged to be dressed in black and to wear a crown, while the Three Dead will have their faces painted fully as skulls. All other attendees are encouraged to paint half of their face like a skull, representing that while living we are also all dying as well. All attendees are to gather in a circle, and the oldest among them is to read the story in the introduction article. (This person will be the narrator.) At the point of the story where the Reaper arrives, the Reaper and his three attendants are to come into the centre of the circle. The Reaper takes up his scythe or pitchfork and stands in the centre while the rest of the story is read. Upon completion of the story, the Three Dead address the narrator:

We Three Dead of yonder graveyard come,
Attending Death to collect our sum,
Just as you are, so once were we,
Just as we are, so shall you be.

The narrator steps forward and says:

We welcome the dead back to receive their share of the first fruits.
Your work contributed to our celebration, and we thank you for that.
Please accept these offerings of the first fruits.

The Three Dead go around the circle carrying baskets, and each attendee places one of the cookies or biscuits into the baskets. If attendees would like to, they may choose to add an image of someone they recently lost as well into the basket to be taken away by the Reaper and his attendants. When the baskets are filled with the cookies, they are placed by the Three Dead at the memento mori altar. The attendees light their little candles and place these at the altar, and all join together in a circle dance.

The following poem is inspired by medieval calendar poems, otherwise known as *monthly labors*, which were mnemonic devices used in the classical and medieval periods to teach about the cycle of the year. This is written as a call and response. The living speak first with the Dead responding (the Deads' responses are in italics). For those in the Southern Hemisphere, simply replace the months to correspond with your local seasons. This can be recited by all those assembled except for the Reaper, who is to remain silent:

At August time we reap the first fruits,
We doth remind the living of their chthonic roots.

In September we work hard in the fields,
While we the dead slumber deep below the yields.

In October we see the dark nights come,
We dance and dance until we are numb.

In November we prepare for the winter ahead,
We welcome those who join our bed.

In December we feast and pray for light,
We revel in the long winter's night.

In January we warm ourselves by the fire,
As we dream of our past lives' desires.

In February we prepare our lands in row,
We bless the oxen and the hoe.

In March we sow the fields with seed,
We watch our children, pleased indeed.

In April new life springs from the womb,
We add new strands to the tapestry loom.

In May we dance around the pole,
We slumber deep within our hole.

In June we celebrate the longest day,
Our bones continue to decay.

In July we watch our crops grow tall,
We anticipate the harvest haul.

The Reaper and the Three Dead take up the baskets and depart the circle, the assembled living all bowing as they leave. A feast follows.

Individual Ritual

For the individual ritual, paint half your face as a skull so that you become part of the living memento mori. Create a memento mori altar for yourself and include a figure of a skeleton to be the embodiment of the Lord of the Harvest. Take on the role of the narrator and recite the story. Upon completion of the story, light candles, which symbolize the arrival of the dead at your ritual, and address the dead collectively:

I welcome the dead back to receive their share of the first fruits. Your work contributed to this celebration, and I thank you for that. Please accept these offerings of the first fruits.

Place each biscuit one by one into a basket in front of the memento mori until all are inside and then recite the call-and-response poem above, but say only the living call, allowing a pause after each call for the dead to respond. To complete the ritual, blow out each of the candles to represent the leaving of the dead.

After the Ritual

The attendee who played the Reaper takes on the task of burying the biscuits and the images of the recently deceased if supplied. Find a suitable place in nature and bury the biscuits, or crumble them and cast the crumbs into a flowing stream. This, in effect, is feeding the actual dead their offering of the fruits of the first harvest by giving them the biscuits. If you performed the ritual yourself, perform this role. Designate a member of the ritual to take the collected offerings to the food bank to share the bounty with the rest of the community.

Notes

Mabon

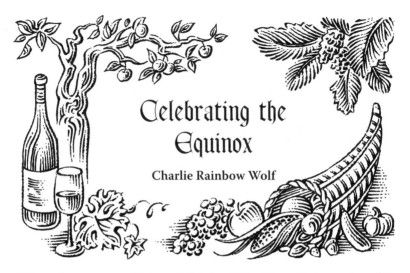

Celebrating the Equinox

Charlie Rainbow Wolf

WHEN I THINK OF Mabon, I think of life. Now, that may be a bit contradictory, because this is the time of year when everything is dying, when the harvest is being gathered, when various trees are preparing to go dormant and some animals are slowing down for hibernation. Usually it is Ostara and Beltane that come to mind when speaking of life and fertility—and rightly so; they are, after all, the growing seasons in the Northern Hemisphere. But how can that life be sustained if the harvest isn't gathered for the winter? Doesn't the very gathering of the harvest celebrate life and its fruits and bounty? Don't we need the seeds from this year's harvest to plant for next year's growth? Of course, it probably helps that my birthday falls near Mabon too!

Harvest Festivals

Harvest was a big thing back when I lived on a farm in England. It was perhaps the busiest time of year. Even though the hay was gathered in the summer—the old adage, "Make hay while the sun shines" was certainly true, for, being an island country, it rained *a lot* over there—I saw the gathering of the hay as the start of the harvest. It was cut as soon as the weather allowed, baled in huge rounds that were then gathered on a spike, and stored in the barn for winter feeding.

After the gathering of hay came the main harvest. We were predominantly an arable farm, and when harvest came, it was all hands on deck. There was an excited buzz throughout the community as people prepared for the harvest festivals. I believe that these festivals have endured for millennia; now their modern versions center on church and school activities.

From September to early October, the villagers decorated the church with harvested items and seasonal flora; services of thanksgiving took place at schools, churches, and other venues; and often the church bell ringers would ring complicated patterns on the church tower bells in celebration of the harvest being gathered for the season. Different villages held their harvest celebrations on different days so that people could travel to celebrate with others without conflicting schedules. It was one of the busiest times for the bell ringers, and I recall ringing at several harvest gatherings during this time. The school usually had a gala day, full of games for the children, followed by a dance for the adults. My memory may be rose colored, but it always seemed that energy was high and people were in good spirits.

Harvest festivals are not unique to England, though. They are celebrated around the world as the harvest is gathered. In the US, the harvest festival has migrated to the Thanksgiving celebrations in late November, but some churches and other institutions still mark the harvest in September, sometimes coinciding with the children returning to school.

Mabon

Even though I left the UK over two decades ago, I witnessed how the harvest festivals had been declining over the years. I wonder if it was due to the abundance of foods found in grocery stores and supermarkets and communities depending less on locally grown produce to get them through the winter. Or maybe the churches were just not offering what the community wanted to experience. I saw the focus shift from harvest to Christmas.

As a practicing Pagan, I keep all of the sabbats. To me, they are all special in their own way. I love the stillness of Imbolc, the bustle of Beltane, and the childlike wonder of Yule. Yet it is Mabon that will forever be the most special to me, partly because of my experiences on the farm, maybe because it is near my solar return, but always because it reminds me to be thankful—and not just for the sabbat, but for each and every moment.

Because of this, we tend to do Mabon in a big way here. I pickle and can and preserve everything I can find, grabbing the last tomatoes out of the garden to make chutney, freezing the last of the peppers to use in soups and stews later, and bringing in rose hips and berries for jams and pies. I'm aware of how fortunate I am to have modern conveniences like the stove and the freezer and running water because I know my ancestors did not. Gratitude is everything.

Deities

Of course the Christian churches devoted their harvest festivals to their god, but in the pantheons of many and varied religious deities, there seem to be innumerable harvest gods and goddesses. I'll give a nod to Lugh, who started the harvest season at Lughnasadh (Lammas) first. He is a Celtic god, one of the Irish Tuatha Dé Danann, and represents craftsmanship and skill. I see Lugh as the bridge between Midsummer (Litha) and Mabon; he's kissed the crops and is waiting for them to ripen to be cut down at his feast of Lughnasadh. But the cutting of the harvest is not the end of the work. It has to be saved and stored, which takes time and effort and energy.

Mabon is actually named after a Celtic god, whose mother was Modron, a goddess of fertility. Mabon and Modron play a reasonable role in Arthurian traditions for those who study them in depth. Rescuing the kidnapped Mabon was one of Arthur's tasks in the *Mabinogion*.

Another very popular Celtic harvest deity is the Dagda. He is the king of the Tuatha Dé Danann, and is associated with agriculture and magic, and is said to influence the weather (and thus the crops), and the seasons. (The Dagda is quite an amazing being; to learn more about him, check out Morgan Daimler's book in the Pagan Portals series.)

Every culture has their own harvest deity. My Cherokee friends honor Selu, the corn mother. In the Greek pantheon, Kronus is a patron of the harvest, and today we see him with his scythe as "Old Father Time." Demeter is the Greek goddess of agriculture and the harvest. The Egyptians honored Osiris as the god of fertility, vegetation, the afterlife, and rebirth. Dan Petro is the Vodou loa who protects farmers. In Norse traditions, it is Freyr who is the god of the harvest and prosperity. The list is extensive, and I've only just scratched the surface, touching on some of the more popular deities.

Don't dismiss a deity just because they are not well known. Someone somewhere had to be the first to interact with the gods. Someone had to be the first to utter their name. A lesser-known deity does not necessarily mean a less powerful one.

Here at the Keep (our name for our little postage stamp we homestead), I tend to honor Rosmerta. She is a lesser-known goddess, and to be honest I'm still finding my way with her. There's little on the web about her (and I don't believe everything I read on the internet). What I do know, based on my personal experiences meshing with what I have read, is that she is a goddess of abundance and plenty, and her symbols are the cornucopia and the offering plate. Some say she's Celtic and some say she's Gallo-Roman. I just know that I can work with her.

She made herself known to me quite by accident. I was on a deadline to meet a pottery order, and with the kiln misbehaving, I wasn't sure that I would complete it. I was so worried about letting a good friend down. At the same time, a family emergency meant my husband had to travel abroad, and only the gods knew when I'd see him again. Due to this situation, I needed an abundance spell sooner rather than later. I put one together, and overnight, several financial emergencies seemed to sort themselves. In meditation I asked who I needed to thank for this, and it was Rosmerta who made herself known to me. Not one to take anything for granted (the gods, thankfully, know I tend to need things in triplicate before I will adhere to something), this was cemented when I turned on my music and the song "Alberta" by Eric Clapton started playing! Now whenever I hear that song, my mind substitutes "Rosmerta" for "Alberta"!

Of course, it is not necessary to work with a harvest deity. If you prefer not to do so, or you have not found one with whom you resonate yet, that's okay. Reach out to Mother Nature by whatever name you choose to call her. She will hear you, and more importantly, she will see your heart. Intention is what matters.

Celebrating the Harvest

I touched on harvest festivals and ways of celebrating the harvest earlier, and by all means if such activities are available and they appeal to you, join in! Big harvest gatherings are not necessary to be thankful for Mabon's bounty, though. Sometimes, because I live in an active farming community, I find myself celebrating Mabon on my own, and that's okay. Whether you work solo or in a group, the main things to remember are the same.

The first is mindfulness. In this day and age, all we have to do is pick up the phone, and before long, hot food is delivered to us effortlessly. But remember, it wasn't always so. You don't have to grow your own food to be mindful of where it came from. You don't even have to cook it yourself to be thankful you have food that is appetizing and just what you were craving. Be mindful of the process: the people who grew and prepared the food, those who were responsible for getting it to you, the technology that made it happen. It's so easy to take things for granted, but being fed should never be one of them.

The second is connection. By taking part in a Mabon feast, you're connecting to so much. You're connecting to the gods and goddesses of your traditions. You're connecting to the earth and what she provides. You're connecting with the ancestors who have celebrated harvests in years gone by. If you're with others, then you're connecting with them in a feast of sharing—not just sharing food but sharing each other's time and energy and experiences. If you're on your own, you're connecting with the deepest part of your inner sanctum, with all those who went before and all those who will come after. This is a very sacred space indeed!

The third is gratitude. We have so much to appreciate, yet sometimes it's easier to complain. It's so easy, though, to flip that headspace into one of appreciation, and doing so often solves many problems. Be thankful for the things that made your harvest possible: the weather, those who worked the fields, those who were instrumental in getting the harvest to your fridge or your stove or your table. As you're mindful of these things, also be grateful for them—even if sometimes they don't go the way you planned. There are far worse things than cold potatoes or the wrong topping on a pizza. If you're working in a group, be thankful for the community, the place to gather, the sharing. If you're working on your own, be thankful for your space, for your quiet time, for the chance to learn and grow. There's always something for which to be thankful.

Further Reading

Guest, Charlotte, trans. *The Mabinogion: Translated from the Red Book of Hergest.* Introduction and footnotes by Owen Edwards. Sandycroft Publishing, 2014.

Daimler, Morgan. *The Dagda: Meeting the Good God of Ireland.* Pagan Portals. Moon Books, 2018.

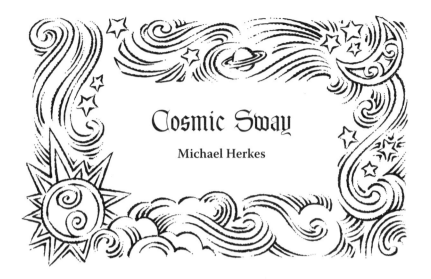

Cosmic Sway

Michael Herkes

As the Wheel of the Year turns, we balance once more between light and dark. Welcome to the season of Mabon, a sabbat that offers a time of gratitude and reflection for all. This stretch from September 22 to October 30, 2026, is packed with potent energies that'll have us all dancing between balance and intensity.

Observing Mabon

We kick things off with Mabon on September 22, which also happens to be the start of Libra season. Now, I don't know about you, but for me, this always feels like the beginning of the season of the witch! There's a crispness in the air, the leaves are starting to turn, and you can almost feel the veil between worlds getting thinner. It's a perfect time for balance work—think about what you need to let go of and what you want to cultivate as we head into the darker half of the year.

For a simple Mabon ritual, try this: Find two leaves—one still green and one that's started to change color. Hold the green leaf and think about what you want to release. Then burn it (safely, please!). Hold the colorful leaf and focus on what you want to bring into your life. Keep this leaf on your altar until Samhain.

Full Moon in Aries

On September 26, we've got a Full Moon in Aries at 12:49 p.m. Aries is fiery, impulsive, and all about action. This is a great time for banishing work or for spells that need an extra boost of energy. You might want to do a ritual to release fears or self-doubt that have been holding you back. Aries doesn't do subtle, so go big with your magic here!

For Aries Full Moon fashion, think bold reds and oranges. Wear something that makes you feel powerful and ready to take on the world.

Venus and Mercury Retrogrades

On October 3, Venus goes retrograde in Scorpio at 3:16 a.m. for about a month, going direct on November 13 at 7:27 p.m. This is a time for reassessing our values, especially in love and money. And with it happening in intense Scorpio, we're talking deep, transformative stuff here. It's a great time for shadow work around relationships. Maybe you've been avoiding looking at some unhealthy patterns or you've been struggling to express your deepest desires. Use this retrograde energy to dive deep and do some serious soul-searching.

But wait, there's more retrograde action in the cosmos! Mercury decides to join the retrograde party on October 24 at 3:13 a.m. until November 13 at 10:54 a.m.

Now, with both Venus and Mercury retrograde in this intense water sign, we're in for some serious communication challenges because of Mercury, but this will be majorly highlighted in our relationships thanks to Venus.

You might find yourself dredging up old issues or misunderstanding your partner's, family's, or even friend's intentions. It's crucial to be extra clear in your communication during this time. Double-check your texts before sending, and try to have important conversations face-to-face if possible.

A protection spell for this double retrograde: Create a sachet with herbs like roses (for protection in relationships) and lavender (for calmness and communication), and carry it with you. Whenever you feel miscommunication brewing, hold the sachet and take a deep breath before responding.

October Moon Magic

October has a New Moon in Libra and a Full Moon in Taurus, putting extra emphasis on Venus, as she rules over both of these signs. We start with a New Moon in Libra on October 10 at 11:50 a.m. Libra energy is all about balance, justice, and relationships. A simple spell for this Moon that coincides with the Venus retrograde is to write a letter to your ideal partner (or your current partner if you're in a relationship), describing the kind of love you want to cultivate. Be honest and vulnerable. Then, burn the letter and visualize the smoke carrying your intentions to Venus.

The Full Moon in Taurus on October 26 at 12:12 a.m. brings earthy, sensual energy. This is a perfect time to focus on self-love and body positivity, as your self-esteem may also be low at this time thanks to the Venus retrograde. I suggest taking a luxurious bath with rose petals and honey. After the bath, gaze at your reflection in a mirror. Lick the index finger of your dominant hand and trace a pentagram onto the surface with your saliva while saying out loud what you enjoy most about yourself to boost your self-confidence.

Summary

Throughout this whole period, from Mabon to Samhain, we're being called to balance opposing energies. We've got the harmony-seeking energy of Libra dancing with the intense, transformative pull of Scorpio. The retrogrades are asking us to look inward and reassess, while the Full Moons are pushing us to release and manifest.

So as you move through this season, don't be afraid to explore all facets of yourself and your practice. Honor the balance of Libra, but also embrace the depth of Scorpio. Work on your relationships, but also stand in your power. Do the deep shadow work that this time calls for, but also celebrate the beauty and abundance of the harvest season.

And most importantly, trust your intuition. The thinning veil makes it easier to receive messages from your guides, ancestors, and your own higher self. Take time to listen. May this season bring you growth, transformation, and a deeper connection to your magical path. Blessed be, witches!

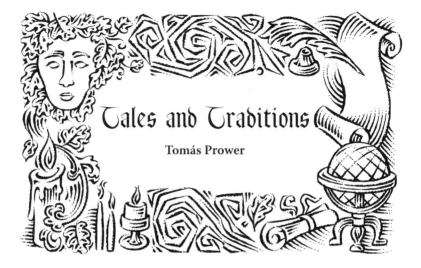

Tales and Traditions

Tomás Prower

MABON IS A DICHOTOMOUS time of year befitting its place as the season of the autumnal equinox. Both balance and disbalance are celebrated features of this sabbat, but which of them gets more attention varies from person to person. Though, ironically, rarely are they given equal attention. Cosmically, Mabon marks the second equinox of the calendar year, when both daylight and nighttime are temporally equal, but unlike its springtime fraternal twin Ostara, Mabon has a more somber tone, a celebration played in a minor key.

On the surface, this is the time of the second harvest, of abundance and thankfulness, but on a deeper, subconscious level, this abundance and thankfulness is in preparation for the dark times ahead. From here on out for the next six months, the darkness will be more powerful than the light, and cold will have strength over warmth. Mabon is a time of taking stock of your achievements and abilities and preparing for the inevitable hard times ahead before they arrive.

Naomi and Ruth: The Balanced Equality of "For Better or for Worse"

It is important to remember that the world is not perfect. There will never be an era of our living years in which we are invulnerable to woe, regardless of if they be small disappointments and setbacks or systemic oppression that steamrolls over ideals like "justice" and "fairness." Life itself is not fair, but it is, paradoxically, also not unfair. Life just is, and an awareness of such makes it more bearable. And thus, Mabon magic is not about stopping the tide of the forces of the Universe. It's not about preventing the inevitability of the next six months of darkness and coldness ahead, nor is it about eliminating all tough times that are stacked like cards among the good times in the deck of fate. Rather, Mabon magic is in mitigation and making those inevitabilities of darkness and tough times less woeful.

In the Bible, more specifically in the Old Testament, there is the story of two inspirational heroines whose courage and love exemplify the lessons of Mabon, both in mitigating the woes of hard times ahead and in the sense of shared equality between lovers. These heroines are known as Naomi and Ruth, and their tale can be found in the appropriately titled "Book of Ruth" within the Bible. Though often forgotten by Christians, Naomi and Ruth still hold a revered place in the hearts of those of the Jewish faith, especially at weddings (for reasons we'll get into), and among progressive Jews in their advocation for same-sex love and marriage.

As their story goes, Naomi is a loving but unremarkable wife and mother of two adult sons. However, when an unrelenting famine strikes her homeland, hunger forces her and her family to flee to the neighboring land Moab, where they try to make a new life for themselves as refugees. Things seem to be going well at first when her sons marry two local Moabite women, but then Naomi's life changes forever as a series of misfortunes strike her. Not only is she made a widow by the death of her beloved husband, but both of her sons also die, all within a short time of one another. Despite the emotional devastation and profound grief Naomi must have been feeling at this time, one would think that at least some comfort could be found in still having her two daughters-in-law by her side, but therein was the crux of Naomi's current and future problems.

Naomi lived in a very different time and culture. Life for a woman in the 1300s BCE in the Middle East was extremely limited compared to modern times in the modern West. Back then and there, women were, for all intents and purposes, considered property, and without a man to provide for them, their economic avenues of prosperity were practically nonexistent, especially for an old woman like Naomi who no longer had physical youth on her side that she could leverage. Thus was Naomi's situation: she was an elderly widow who had to wholly rely on her daughters-in-law for economic support, knowing full well that they couldn't even support themselves unless they did things they didn't want to do and which would only stigmatize them further. And so, in a symbolic act of "harvest," Naomi altruistically reaps herself out of her daughters-in-laws' lives, mandating that they return to their original families and find new husbands while youth was still on their side. This act was essentially suicidal for Naomi, but she and her daughters-in-law knew that it was the only way for the two young women to have the future possibility of a happy life.

Upon receiving Naomi's blessing to abandon her so as to avoid a future of certain hardship, one of the daughters-in-law is incredibly relieved and does, indeed, leave. The other daughter-in-law, however, was Ruth, and she refused to abandon her mother-in-law, come what may. Ruth had no plans as to how she and Naomi would overcome the dark times ahead since, after all, as a widow herself, Ruth's chances of marriage were nonoptimal since she was no longer virginal, but she just had supreme faith that, together, she and Naomi could handle the future, supported only by their love for one another. Both of them knew they couldn't prevent the tough times ahead, but, together, they could mitigate them through having each other.

In modern times, Ruth's passionate declaration of staying by Naomi's side, aware of the hard life ahead because of this decision, is an oft-quoted scriptural passage in Jewish wedding ceremonies. And the semantic nuances of Hebrew in the scripture heavily implies a marital type of love between the two women, the same words having been used in previous Bible stories when expressing romantic love between heterosexual couples.

Still, ritualistic use and scholarly insight aside, Naomi and Ruth's determination to make their respective futures better by helping each other is a main lesson of Mabon. Neither try to combat the hard times ahead, nor do they try to avoid them. They are aware of the inevitable and simply try to mitigate the impending harshness and sorrow by loving and being there for each other now more than ever. Ultimately, their bond prevails, and Ruth goes on to remarry a wonderful man who helps care for an aging Naomi, and so, too, can you have a happy ending when the cold and darkness recede. But until then, don't waste your energy fighting the inevitable. Reap your harvest, share it with those in need, and together, we'll all make the winter of our lives a little warmer and brighter.

Feasts and Treats

Nathan M. Hall

THE AUTUMN EQUINOX HAS arrived, and with it, thoughts of gathering in, pulling close together with our families and families of choice. It might still be warm, but we know cool nights are ahead, and the turning of the wheel to the golden colors of fall is upon us.

Mabon Salad

Rich beets and goat cheese pair well with the sharp edge of arugula and radishes in this recipe. It's a perfect offering for the equinox when warm days are followed by crisp evenings.

Prep time: 20 minutes
Cooking time: 40 minutes
Servings: 6

2 golden or red beets
4 tablespoons olive oil
1 teaspoon sea salt, or more to taste
5 ounces arugula (Packages labeled baby arugula will be a bit more
    tender.)
3 radishes, sliced thin
4-ounce package goat cheese, cut into chunks
2 tablespoons red wine vinegar

Fresh ground pepper

½ teaspoon oregano

½ cup shelled pistachios, slightly crushed and preferably unsalted

Preheat oven to 400°F and, using a fork, prick the skin of the beets all around. Place them on a sheet of aluminum foil and drizzle with 1–2 tablespoons of the olive oil and salt before closing the foil around them and popping into the oven for about 40 minutes. A fork should easily slide into the beets when they're ready. Give them more time in the oven if they're still too firm.

Assemble the salad in a large bowl with arugula, sliced radishes, and chunks of goat cheese. Whisk together the remaining olive oil, vinegar, salt, pepper, and oregano for the dressing.

When the beets are ready, open the foil and let stand and cool for about 10 minutes. Under running water, rub the skins of the beets; they should easily slide off. With a paring knife, cut off the root end of each beet and then cut in half and slice. If any of the skin remained, make sure to cut it off as well. Place the sliced beets on the salad and top with pistachios. When you're ready to serve, pour the dressing over the top and toss to mix well.

Focaccia Bread

Focaccia bread is deceptively easy to make and a hearty accompaniment to the salad, making for a satisfying meal.

Prep time: 15 minutes

Rising time: 1 hour and 20 minutes

Cooking time: 8–10 minutes

Servings: 8

1 cup warm water

1 tablespoon active dry yeast

1 teaspoon brown sugar

410 grams flour (I like to measure flour out by weight for better precision. This comes out to about 3 cups.)

2 tablespoons olive oil, plus more for drizzling on top after the
  dough is spread out in the pan

1 teaspoon granulated sea salt

2 teaspoons crushed rosemary

2 teaspoons sea salt flakes to sprinkle on top (Maldon is a good
  brand)

In a stand mixer, pour in about a quarter of the cup of warm water, yeast, and brown sugar. Stir well with a fork and let stand for about 10 minutes until the yeast wakes up and creates a nice foamy layer. Pour in the remaining ¾ cup of warm water and add all of the remaining ingredients except the sea salt flakes.

Using the dough hook attachment, knead the dough until it comes together in a nice ball. Pour 2 tablespoons olive oil into a large bowl, making sure to coat all the sides. With wet hands, remove the dough ball from the mixer and place into the large bowl. Cover with plastic wrap and leave to rise in a warm place for about an hour.

When the hour is up, preheat the oven to 500°F. Line a ⅛-size sheet pan (6 × 9 inches) with parchment paper and a thin layer of olive oil. Take the dough out, which should have doubled in size, and work it into the sheet pan, rolling it out with your hands into an even layer that fills the pan. With your fingertips, poke straight down repeatedly all over the dough to create divots, and drizzle with more olive oil. Sprinkle the sea salt flakes generously over the top and let rise for another 20 minutes or so while waiting for the oven to come to temperature.

Place in the hot oven for 8–10 minutes, until the bread rises and turns a beautiful golden brown. Remove and let cool slightly on a rack before slicing into 8 pieces, serving while still warm.

Classic Apple Pie

In my family, we used to have an apple orchard, and while it's long gone now, there's still nothing that symbolizes fall to me like an apple pie.

Prep time: 25 minutes
Chilling time: 1 hour to overnight
Cooking time: 45 minutes–1 hour
Servings: 8

Pie crust (makes 2 crusts)

400 grams flour (About 3 cups, but I like to measure the flour in this recipe by weight.)
2 tablespoons granulated sugar
1 tablespoon kosher salt
2½ sticks cold butter, cut into cubes
1 cup ice water

Pie filling

2 tablespoons butter
⅓ cup sugar
4 large apples, peeled, cored, and sliced (Braeburn, Honeycrisp, or Granny Smith)
2 tablespoons water, plus 1 tablespoon for cornstarch slurry
1 tablespoon flour
1 teaspoon cinnamon
½ teaspoon allspice
¼ teaspoon nutmeg, freshly grated
3 teaspoons cornstarch

For the pie crust: In a food processor, mix the flour, sugar, and salt. Drop in the cold butter cubes a couple at a time, using the pulse function on the processor to break them apart before adding a few more. Slowly drizzle in about half of the water while continuing to pulse. Keep pulsing until the dough has formed into small, gravel-sized pieces and there's no more loose flour. If necessary, dribble in more water a tablespoon at a time, but don't overdo it.

When the dough is crumbly, drop it onto a floured work surface and gently knead it together. You want it to just come together, so don't overwork it. Separate into two balls and place each onto a sheet of plastic wrap. With a rolling pin, quickly flatten into two discs and then close the plastic wrap around them. Again with the rolling pin, roll out the discs so that they completely fill the plastic wrap—this will help them stick together later. Put the two discs in the refrigerator for at least an hour or preferably overnight.

For the pie filling: Heat a large saucepan over medium heat. Melt the butter and sugar together and then add the apples. Sprinkle in the water, flour, cinnamon, allspice, and nutmeg and stir. Cover and let cook until the apples start to soften. Mix the 1 tablespoon of water and cornstarch together, then slowly add to pan, stirring until mixed in. When the apples are soft but not breaking apart, remove from heat and allow to cool completely.

To make the pie: Preheat the oven to 375°F.

Take one portion of the dough out of the refrigerator and roll it out on a floured surface large enough to fit nicely in a 9-inch metal pie pan with a little overhang. Put the cooled apple mixture inside and grab the other half of the dough and roll it out, placing on top of the pie. Cut off the overhang and pinch together the two crusts, then crimp with your fingers all around the perimeter. Using a paring knife, cut a few vents in the top to vent steam. Bake for 45 minutes to an hour, when the crust is golden brown and the filling is visibly bubbling in the steam vents. Use a pie shield or some aluminum foil to protect the edge of the crust if it's getting too brown too quickly.

Cool on a wire rack and serve when still warm.

Chai Latte

There are certainly more traditional ways to make chai lattes, but this is a quick and dirty version that gets the job done.

Prep time: 5 minutes
Cooking time: 20 minutes
Servings: 4

2 cups water
1 cinnamon stick

5 cardamom pods, lightly crushed

8–10 black peppercorns, lightly crushed

2–3 cloves

3 tablespoons black tea

2 tablespoons brown sugar

2 cups whole milk, or milk substitute

Bring the water, cinnamon, cardamom, peppercorns, and cloves to a boil and reduce to low heat. Allow to simmer for 10 minutes (or longer) with a lid on top. Add in the loose black tea and continue simmering for another 10 minutes or so. With a fine mesh strainer, separate out the liquid from the solids and return the liquid to the pan. Add in brown sugar and stir until dissolved. Add in the milk or milk substitute, stirring while pouring, and continue to stir until hot.

Serve in teacups with the apple pie and enjoy.

Crafty Crafts

Raechel Henderson

MABON SEES US STARTING to close up our homes and hunker down for the coming colder months. It is a time of taking stock of what we have and what we need to get before we can truly enjoy the fall. The sabbat's energy is all about prosperity, balance, and protection. We start closing up our doors and windows, which can trap stagnant energy. Before you close up completely, consider using the smoke cleansing bundles that you made back in Beltane to clear out any negative or stale energy. Then you can bless the space and protect it with a witch ball.

Witch Ball

Witch balls are believed to have originated in seventeenth- and eighteenth-century England. They were hung in windows, and their purpose was to protect the home from evil spirits, evil spells, bad luck, and, of course, witches. While they may be of more modern origins, the balls work much like witch bottles by distracting and then trapping any evil spirits or spellwork.

The beauty of a witch ball is twofold. First, it is practical. Being able to hang something in your window that you can then mostly forget about frees up your thinking for other magical tasks. But second, it is also physically beautiful, especially if you take the time to decorate the outside of the ball with protective charms and sigils.

A witch ball can be easily made using the refillable ball ornaments that are meant for Christmas trees. Unscrew the top of the ornament, fill it with various *materia magica*, close it up, and hang it in a window where it will work to keep your house safe. Some paths and practices replace the witch ball every year. I think this is a good idea, as well as keeping your witch ball regularly dusted.

Choose protective herbs like basil, cinnamon, clove, clover, juniper, lavender, or rosemary. For crystals, go with jet, obsidian, amethyst, smoky quartz, or black tourmaline. You can use any number of herbs or crystals in your witch ball. When it comes to crystals, stick with chips and smaller ones so they can fit inside the ball.

Materials
Empty ball ornament
Sea salt
Herbs, 3 different kinds
Crystals, 3 different kinds or 3 pieces of one type
Needles and pins
Twine or ribbon
Optional: rose thorns, cactus needles, pentacle, nazar, biodegradable glitter, bells, charms

Tools
Funnel
Scissors
Optional: paints or markers
> *Cost:* $10–$20
> *Time spent:* 30 minutes

Instructions
Create sacred space to work in according to your path. Gather your materials. You'll want to give them a good cleansing with your preferred method. If you don't have one, I recommend using sound:

ring a bell around the materials to break up and disperse any energies that might be clinging to them.

As you are assembling your witch ball, envision each material working as its role dictates. The salt grounds, the herbs and crystals protect, the needles stop, etc. You might even give thanks to each as you add them to the ball. They will be working hard to protect you in the future, so gratitude isn't out of place.

Start by adding your sea salt using the funnel. The sea salt grounds the energy captured by the witch ball and helps hold it in place. While sea salt is suggested for this craft, you can use regular table salt in a pinch.

Next, add your herbs. Using a combination of three is suggested, as that is a magical number of increase, which will amplify the power of the herbs. This same logic extends to your crystals, although if you only have one, you can still tap into the power of three by adding three of the same kind.

Once you have added your crystals, you will need to insert your pins or needles into the ball. Use three, five, or seven pins, as those are odd numbers, which have the power of disruption. The pins and needles will act as a barrier to negative energy or malicious magic, catching it before it has a chance to enter your space. This same function can be performed by rose thorns or cactus needles if you prefer.

You can add other items to your witch ball if you wish. Apotropaic charms such as a pentacle or nazar can aid in repelling any malicious energy. Biodegradable glitter can act in the same capacity, with the added benefit of breaking up the energy in its reflective surfaces.

Once you have filled your witch ball, cap it with the top. You can now decorate your ball with paints or markers if you wish. Add a painting of eyes to deflect the evil eye or draw protective runes such as Algiz on the outside of the ornament. Add bells to the outside or any charms that were too big to fit inside the ball. If you do so, think about what protection means to you and visualize what it will look like when your witch ball takes in that malicious, negative energy that tries to find its way into your home.

Before you finish your ball, you need to charge it. Tell it that its mission is to protect your home, allowing nothing to enter your home that would wish to harm you. Run a piece of twine or ribbon through the ornament's top and hang the witch ball in your window.

Keep your witch ball dusted so that it stays in optimal working condition. A good time to do so is on the waning moon to clear away any stale surface energy that might have settled on it with the dust. When you are cleaning your witch ball, take some time to examine the contents. If you see any discoloration, mold, or other signs of decay inside, that indicates the witch ball has taken on a large amount of negative energy and needs to be replaced. The same goes for if the ball is cracked or damaged in any way. In either case, dispose of the herbs and salt either by throwing them into a garbage outside of your home or burying them. You can even flush those materials down the toilet.

The crystals, pins, and any charms can be cleansed with smoke, salt, or water and then reused. If the ball hasn't been harmed, it can be reused as well as long as you cleanse it. At least once a year you'll want to change out the contents of your witch ball and remake it.

Mabon
Meditations

Elizabeth Barrette

WITH AUTUMN COMES COOLING temperatures and the hustle of field work before everything goes dormant for winter. Mabon celebrates the abundance of harvest now that crops are securely in storage. This is a good time to work on gratitude meditations to give thanks for all that you have. Lots of people count their blessings at this time of year. Many autumn rituals and festivals feature drumming, and dancing is popular too. This type of meditation, based on sound and motion, may appeal to more active folks who quickly get bored with the quiet versions.

Gratitude Meditation

Mindfulness can direct attention to what you have. A gratitude meditation helps you appreciate those things more. By focusing on what you already have, you reduce the desire to pursue more and more. It makes you more content with things as they are now.

Gratitude meditation increases feelings of happiness and well-being. It increases your optimism, which makes it easier to take a chance on trusting strangers. It improves your compassion for yourself and other people. It lifts your everyday mood and bolsters your ability to see the good more than the bad. That reduces the time you spend worrying.

Gratitude meditation can even alter your brain in ways that improve your ability to deal with challenges in the future. If you have suffered serious hardships in the past, it supports post-traumatic growth moving forward. The point is not to forget or ignore the bad things that have happened, or are happening, but rather to reduce your distress over them so you can cope better. Your positive experiences and resources form a buffer.

The more you practice gratitude, the more your perspective changes. You gain better control over how you feel and how you view a situation. This influences what you consider negative, neutral, or positive. When you see more positives than negatives, you feel happier. You learn to cope with what you cannot change, work on changing what you can, and examine things with a clear mind to tell which is which—what some people call "rock problems" and "clay problems."

For a gratitude meditation, find a comfortable place to sit. You can close your eyes or leave them open. A focal object works well here—something you treasure, such as a wedding ring or a key to your home. Breathe slowly and deeply. Attend to your breath as you relax. Now turn your attention to how you feel in this moment. Think about your present circumstances and your body, what you appreciate about them. Consider the past and what within it has helped you achieve your present state. Turn your attention to the future and any plans or opportunities you are looking forward to. Go down a list if you need to: your family, friends, and pets; your home and favorite places; your job, coworkers, hobbies, and playmates; your life, health, and body. Think of the turning seasons and what you enjoy at this time of year, like upcoming holidays or fun activities.

If you struggle to "think up" things that make you grateful on demand, consider carrying a gratitude journal with you. Whenever something good happens during the day, you can pause for a moment of thankfulness as you write it down. Then, reading each day's notes of appreciation can become part of your evening meditation session. You might take five minutes in the morning to give thanks for stable things in your life, such as your home, loved ones, and job. Then set aside five minutes in the evening to remember positive things that happened during your day.

Drumming Meditation

A drumming meditation is a good choice for people who have strong musical or kinesthetic leanings. It's a way of moving while sitting still and making meaningful sound without speaking. It unites the mind, body, and spirit. Thus, it appears in many magical and spiritual traditions around the world.

If you're not good at focusing on your breath, this is a great technique for you, because it doesn't involve that. Instead you focus on the drum and its rhythm. Playing the drum creates a positive feedback loop in your mind and body. It connects with the heartbeat—the first rhythm we encountered on incarnating in this life. Similarly, the drum is among the oldest musical instruments, so it speaks to deep time and can help connect with the ancestors.

Drumming meditation integrates the different parts of your brain so that they work together more fluently. This boosts both intuitive and logical functions. As you practice, you also improve your cognitive performance overall. If you drum in a group, you can create a kind of shared consciousness that strengthens your connection with other people. Because it releases endorphins and gives you something physical to focus on, drumming boosts pain tolerance. It can also reduce blood pressure.

Think about what kind of drum you want to play while meditating. A hand drum such as bongos or a doumbek gives you the most physical feedback as the vibrations travel through your body. There are many small, round drums that are held in the hand and hit with a stick. A wooden drumstick gives a sharper sound, good for commanding attention; a padded one gives a softer sound that is less jarring. Then there are a few oddballs, like the bodhrán, whose stick is sort of rolled across the surface and may prove more complicated to play than ideal for this purpose. Some very large drums are meant to be played by multiple people together, which makes a terrific group meditation.

Ideally, you need a quiet place for the drumming meditation. You don't want other sounds to interfere with the beat. Conversely, it should be somewhere private or at least soundproofed. You don't want to bother other people, especially if they are attempting a quieter form of meditation. However, drumming meditation combines splendidly with dancing, should anyone wish to try that as a moving meditation.

For this practice, forget standard meditation poses and sit to hold the drum comfortably. You may need a chair, and for a large drum, you may need a stand also. You probably don't need a music stand and pages, unless you are attempting one of the fancier "trance dance" rhythms. Most meditative drumming is simple. You just make a heartbeat rhythm and keep it steady. Focus on the feel of playing and the sound coming from the drum. Let it pound everything else out of your awareness. Feel yourself awakening and coming to enlightenment as the rhythm flows through you, raising you to a higher level of consciousness.

At harvest time, pay attention to how you raise and gather energy. Gratitude and drumming are just the beginning of what you can do. After a year of practice, you should have a good grasp of meditation techniques and self-awareness. Watch for new ideas to try in the year to come.

Mabon Ritual

Charlie Rainbow Wolf

THIS IS A PARTICIPATION ritual that can be combined with the festival feast—in fact, it seems to work very well when the two are blended! It can be done alone or in a group setting, either indoors or outside. It's whatever you choose, however you want to make it happen.

Feasting On Abundance

What I'm providing are loose guidelines for the Mabon ritual that I do here. I believe that ritual should be deeply personal, so please feel free to adapt this outline as you desire or require.

The tools are very simple: the main thing you're going to need is a basket, cornucopia, or a large plate. Being a potter, I tend to make a ritual plate, but there's nothing wrong with buying one or even using paper plates if they're more convenient for you! You're also going to need pen and paper for everyone involved, even if you're doing this alone. You'll also want a table (the more people attending, the bigger the table needs to be). It should be able to hold whatever foods people are bringing as well as the central offering plate.

I'm big on ritual fires. I have a firepit in the yarden (yard + garden = yarden), but a pit is not necessary. A candle will do, even a small tealight. For me, I find it easier to connect to the gods and goddesses in liminal spaces like candlelight, twilight, or the light from a bonfire, but again, do what feels right to you. I cannot stress this enough. Bonfire or tealight, just ensure there's a flame there.

Next, you'll want some water. You don't have to go to a sacred well for it; any potable water is fine. If you're working on your own, you might just want to grab a glass of tap water. If you're doing this with others, maybe suggest people bring a bottle of water or water from their own faucet in clean containers. You'll also need a jug or a pitcher to collect some of this water too.

A knife is also required. This doesn't have to be a ritual sword (although we have used that in the past and it was rather fun to do so), but it does need to be fairly sharp, as it will be cutting food. If you have a favorite ritual knife, this is a good time to use it; if not, a kitchen carving or paring knife will suffice.

Finally, think about what you're going to feast on, for that is the main part of this ritual! You've worked hard and gathered in your harvest. Even if you work in an office and exchange that energy in the form of money to acquire your food, you've still worked hard to harvest it! Remember the connection part of this ritual. See how it all goes together? For those working alone, gather up some of your favorite autumnal foods and ensure at least one piece has some kind of seeds in it. (I frequently use an apple; it's easy to obtain and the seeds are obvious in the core.) If there is going to be a group of people, it's a good idea to try to organize the food so that not everyone brings the same thing. (We once had three pots of mac and cheese and very little else at one of our gatherings.)

Our rituals are very low key and small. We don't stand on high ceremony with the gods and the ancestors and the otherkin. Fortunately, they seem to understand that we're human and sometimes make mistakes, because so far we have not been chastened. Large or small, your ritual is *your* devotion, and whatever feels right to you is what is right for you. If it is your custom to gather into a formal opening and call your quarters and put up your wards and whatever else is your normal practice, then the time to do that is after everyone has arrived and put their contribution to the food on the table.

Once the ceremony has been opened and the fire or candle has been lit, it's time to call in the harvest deities being honored. I usually say something like:

I call to the elements of the harvest, to the gods and goddesses that made it possible. I call to the high ones and those who have ascended. I call to the ancestors, those who have gone before and those who are yet to come. I call to the elemental kingdoms, the otherkin, and all good beings to hear my words. Thank you for the bounty we have received. Thank you for the good things that are yet to come. Thank you for gracing us with your presence. Join our feast should you care to do so. You are most welcome at this table.

Before eating, I write down what I am most thankful for (hence the need for paper and pen). If others are with me, I have them do the same, and then we "feed the fire" and let it consume our gratitude. If you're only working with a candle, you can still do this, but make sure to burn the paper safely, maybe over the sink if you are inside (and use a sticky note rather than a big sheet of paper).

Next, have everyone pour some of their water into the jug or pitcher. Before the pandemic, we used to share this, drinking from a chalice. Now, after we have all added our water to the jug, we pour some of it from the jug back into our own receptacles again and share the water that way. For those who still feel uncomfortable about drinking what has been shared, they can offer their water to the ground as refreshment for the soil. After all, the crops of tomorrow won't grow without rain!

Now, it's time to feast! Remember the offering plate? Everyone takes a small piece of whatever food they brought and they put it on the offering plate, using the blade to cut it. The seeds are also put on the plate. This represents gratitude for and sharing of what we have now and thankfulness for the seeds that will provide next year's harvest. This is also an appropriate time to add wild birdseed to the ritual plate—the next paragraph will explain why.

At the end of the fellowship, the offering plate is left outside. Please ensure that all foods on the plate are safe for the wildlife who may have access to it, and if in doubt, scrape the contents of the plate into the ritual fire or dispose of the food on it respectfully. If there are doubts about whether the food is safe or not, perhaps just leave a bit of birdseed on the plate.

I leave my offering plate on the well cap for the water spirit (the Well Hag). Yes, I know it's probably the nighttime critters who come and take the food, and I'm okay with that. Everything is so intrinsically connected here. How wonderful it is to be aware of the kinship!

Notes

Notes

Notes

Notes